# *The Crown of Life*

*HARCOURT BRACE JOVANOVICH, PUBLISHERS*

*San Diego New York London*

# The Crown of Life

## ARTISTIC CREATIVITY IN OLD AGE

## Hugo Munsterberg

Requests for permission to make copies of any
part of the work should be mailed to: Permissions,
Harcourt Brace Jovanovich, Publishers, 757 Third Avenue,
New York, NY 10017

Library of Congress Cataloging in Publication Data
Munsterberg, Hugo, 1916–
The crown of life.
Bibliography: p.
Includes index.
1. Aged as artists.   2. Artists—Biography.
I. Title.
N8356.A43M86   1983     704'.0565     82–21162
ISBN 0-15-623202-2 (A Harvest/HBJ book)

Designed by Joy Chu
Printed in the United States of America
First edition
B C D E

This Book is dedicated to the memory of
BILL TRAYLOR
who was born a slave in Alabama
took up painting at eighty-five
and became a fine
American folk artist.

# Contents

Illustrations   *ix*
Acknowledgments   *xiii*
Introduction   *1*

1. A Distinct Style in Old Age   *11*
2. The Last Is the Best   *54*
3. Never Too Late to Begin   *81*
4. The Work Goes On . . .   *95*
5. Past the Peak   *168*
6. Enough Is Enough   *184*
7. And into Their Nineties . . .   *192*
8. The Crown of Life   *203*

Bibliography   *209*
Index   *211*

# *Illustrations*

Michelangelo Buonarroti, *Pietà*, 1500   *16*
Michelangelo Buonarroti, *Pietà*, 1550–55   *16*
Titian, *Rape of Europa*, 1560   22
Donatello, *Lamentation*, 1450   25
Rembrandt van Rijn, *Lucretia*, 1664   28
El Greco, *Opening of the Fifth Seal*, 1610–14   *31*
Frans Hals, Male Portrait, 1650–52   *33*
Francisco Goya, *Two Old Men
   Eating Their Soup*, 1818–19   35
Francisco Goya, *Saturn Devouring
   His Son*, 1820–22   *36*
Joseph Mallord William Turner, *Burning of the
   Houses of Parliament*, 1834   40
Claude Monet, *Water Lilies*, 1920   *44*
Paul Cézanne, *Le Chateau Noir*, 1904   *48*
Henri Matisse, *Beasts of the Sea*, 1950   *51*
Katsushika Hokusai,
   *The Kirifuri Waterfall*, 1823–30   57

Tomioka Tessai, *Mountain Landscape*, c. 1907   59
Christian Rohlfs, *Yucca*, 1930s   65
Pierre Bonnard, *Dining Room on the Garden*,
   before 1933   66
Julius Bissier, *12 Dez 61 Aquarell*, 1961   70
Richard Lindner, *Ice*, 1966   73
Louise Nevelson, *Expanding Reflection
   Zag II*, 1977   75
Louise Nevelson, Chapel of the
   Good Shepherd, 1976   76
Louis Kahn, Kimbell Art Museum,
   Fort Worth, Texas, 1974   78
Louis Kahn, Kimbell Art Museum,
   Fort Worth, Texas, interior   79
Grandma Moses, *Black Horses*, 1942   83
Morris Hirshfield, *Girl In a Mirror*, 1940   85
Louis Vivin, *Church of St. Laurent and
   the Gare de l'Est*, c. 1922   88
Alfred Wallis, *Schooner under the Moon*,
   1935–36   89
Uragami Gyokudo, *Sanchu Dankin*, c. 1810   92
Sengai, *Shoki*, 1820s   93
Giovanni Bellini, *The Feast of the Gods*, 1513   96
Paolo Uccello, *The Hunt at Night*, 1469   98
Andrea Mantegna, *Judith and
   Holofernes*, 1495   99
Luca Signorelli, *Calvary*, 1505   100
Lucas Cranach, *Venus*, 1532   101
Tintoretto, *Bacchus and Ariadne*, 1578   102
Luca della Robbia, *Adoration of the
   Magi*, c. 1472   104
Giovanni Lorenzo Bernini,
   Piazza di San Pietro, 1656–65   105
Nicolas Poussin, *Blind Orion Searching for
   the Rising Sun*, 1658   108
Claude Lorrain, *Apollo and the Muses on
   Mount Parnassus*, 1674   110

Sir Christopher Wren, St. Paul's Cathedral,
   1675–1710 *111*

Jean Baptiste Siméon Chardin,
   *Still Life With Wild Duck*, 1764 *113*

Alessandro Magnasco, *Landscape with*
   *Boat and Fisherman*, 1735–40 *114*

Giovanni Battista Tiepolo,
   *Apollo Pursuing Daphne*, 1755–60 *115*

Francesco Guardi, *Campo San Zanipolo*, 1782 *117*

J. H. Füssli (Fuseli), *Murdered Woman and*
   *Furies*, 1821 *118*

J. A. Gabriel, Petit Trianon, 1762–68 *120*

Thomas Jefferson, Monticello, 1820–26 *120*

Jacques Louis David, *Cupid and Psyche*, 1817 *123*

J.A.D. Ingres, *Comtesse d'Haussonville*, 1845 *124*

William Blake, *When The Morning Stars*
   *Sang Together*, 1826 *125*

Jean-Baptiste Camille Corot,
   *Gypsy Girl with a Mandolin*, 1870–5 *127*

Pierre Auguste Renoir, *Tilla Durieux*, 1914 *128*

Edgar Degas, *Developpé en Avant*, c. 1915 *129*

Winslow Homer, *Palm Tree, Nassau*, 1898 *131*

Thomas Eakins, *Mrs. Edith Mahon*, 1904 *132*

John Nash, Royal Pavilion, Brighton, 1815–21 *134*

Sesshu, *Landscape in the Cursive Style*, 1496 *137*

Wen Cheng-ming, *The Seven*
   *Thuja Trees*, 1532 *138*

Wang Hui, *The Wisteria Studio*, 1712 *139*

Chu Ta, *Birds and Lotus Pond*, 1690 *140*

Tao-chi, *The Peach Blossom Spring*, c. 1700 *141*

Hakuin, *Monkey Reaching for Reflection of*
   *Moon*, c. 1760 *142*

Frank Lloyd Wright, Guggenheim Museum,
   New York City, 1949–59 *144*

Frank Lloyd Wright, Guggenheim Museum,
   New York City, interior *144*

Le Corbusier, Notre-Dame-du-Haut, 1950–55 *147*

Mies van der Rohe, Seagram Building,
    New York City, 1958    *149*
Georges Braque, *The Wash Stand*, 1944    *151*
Fernand Léger, *The Great Parade*, 1954    *152*
Wassily Kandinsky, *Ribbon with Squares*, 1944    *154*
Piet Mondrian, *Broadway Boogie-Woogie*, 1943    *155*
Edward Hopper, *Second-Story Sunlight*, 1960    *156*
Mark Tobey, *Mystery of the Light*, 1969    *157*
Lyonel Feininger, *Early Steamer*, c. 1955    *158*
Josef Albers, *Homage to the
    Square—Frontal Backing*, 1970    *159*
Aristide Maillol, *The River*, 1943    *160*
Constantin Brancusi, *King of Kings*, 1937    *161*
Hans Arp, *Seuil Configuration*, c. 1960    *162*
Jacques Lipchitz, *Bellerophon Taming
    Pegasus*, 1973    *165*
Henry Moore, *Reclining Figure*, 1963–65    *166*
Rufino Tamayo, *Hombre Sonriente*, 1977    *167*
Raphael Soyer, *Deborah*, 1977    *167*
Maria Martinez, Pottery Jar, 1940s    *193*
Sonia Delaunay, *Ellipse*, 1969    *195*
Jose de Creeft, *Amor, 1973*, 1973    *197*
Ch'i Pai-shih, *Flowers*, 1949    *201*

# Acknowledgments

This book would not have been possible without the work of many scholars, some among the living, others dead, who have done research on the lives and careers of the artists discussed. To all of them, those who are specifically quoted in the text and those whose studies were used for reference, I wish to express my thanks. I am also deeply indebted to the collectors, museums, and dealers who, as on previous occasions, so generously made photographs of works in their possession available to me, especially The Metropolitan Museum of Art, the National Gallery of Art in Washington, D.C., The Museum of Modern Art, and The Solomon R. Guggenheim Museum. Finally, I am deeply indebted to my assistants Mary Prevo and Lauren Zadro, whose contributions in research, editing, and typing the material were invaluable, and to my wife, whose advice and aid, as on many previous occasions, proved of great help.

# The Crown of Life

# Introduction

As life expectancy increases and more and more people reach the biblical age of three score and ten years, the problem of old age becomes ever more important. A great many studies have dealt with its medical and physiological aspects, while others have discussed the economic and sociological consequences, but very little attention has been paid to the question of creativity in the advanced years of human life. It is to this aspect that this book addresses itself, with special emphasis upon the visual artist in old age, a period when some of the greatest figures produced their best work and sometimes even developed a distinctive old-age style, while others, having exhausted themselves, either petered out or stopped creating altogether.

Just what constitutes old age and when it begins has been a matter of controversy for hundreds of years, and opinions have varied greatly at different eras and in different civilizations. Shakespeare spoke of the seven ages of man, reflecting an ancient tradition that goes back to biblical times. The Greek philosopher Solon divided human life into ten stages, each of which lasted seven years, while Aristotle recognized only three periods: youth, the prime of life, and old age. He did not put a specific time limit on any of them, which is very wise, since obviously these phases vary not only in individual persons but also in different periods and cultures. In our modern Western civilization, however, there is no doubt that old age begins somewhere between sixty and seventy, when most people retire from the active pursuits of their earlier life, although a few exceptional individuals undertake new and challenging careers.

In primitive societies there are many different points of view about old age and the role of the elderly. Some tribes give the aged important positions because they respect their wisdom and experience, while others see them as a burden to be eliminated as soon as possible. In *The Role of the Aged in Primitive Society*, Leo Simmons cites many cultures in which men and women were highly regarded for their skill in crafts as well as for knowledge of legends and traditions; the Eskimos, in contrast, exposed their aged to death by freezing when they were no longer strong enough to keep up with the movements of the group. He ends his discussion by saying, "In final summary, it can be stated explicitly that in primitive societies aged men and women have been generally regarded as repositories of knowledge and imparters of valuable information, as specialists in dealing with certain aleatory elements and they have supervised and instructed the arts and crafts."[1]

In the classical world, the attitude toward the elderly is probably best expressed in Cicero's famous *De Senectute*, one of the most profound and eloquent statements on the nature of old age. In it he says,

> From a more general point of view, it seems to me that once we have had our fill of all the things that have engaged our interest, we have had our fill of life itself. There are interests that are proper to childhood: does a full-grown man regret their loss? There are interests that belong to early manhood: when we reach full maturity in what is called "middle age"—do we look back to them with longing? Middle age itself has its special concerns, even these have lost their attractions for the old. Finally, there are interests peculiar to old age; these fall

[1] Leo Simmons, *The Role of the Aged in Primitive Society* (New Haven: Yale University Press, 1945), p. 175.

away too, just as did those of earlier years. When this happens, a sense of fullness of life tells us that it is time to die.[2]

Other classical writers took an equally positive view of old age. To give an example, in Euripides' *Phoemissae*, Jocasta says, "Not all is contemptible in age . . . experience has something to say, indeed, wiser than the young man's words." In fact, the general image in antiquity is that of the wise old seer or poet whose insights are far more profound than that of younger men and women who lack life's experience and are less attuned to the ways of the gods.[3]

An even more positive view was traditionally held in the Orient, especially in China, where Confucianism venerated the aged and saw the ancient sages as the very embodiment of wisdom and moral perfection. Confucius himself expresses this concept when he says: "At fifteen I began to be seriously interested in study. At thirty I formed my character. At forty I had no more perplexities. At fifty I knew the will of heaven. At sixty nothing that I heard disturbed me. At seventy I could let my thought wander without trespassing the law."[4]

To become a sage who had transcended the passions and storms of life, to live in peace with one's self and one's fellowmen, to enjoy the esteem and love of the young, these were ideals that for centuries governed a large part of the human race in eastern Asia and which still exert a powerful influence today.

While Westerners have never looked upon old age with the serenity of the Chinese, there have been many outstanding Europeans who have regarded it as a meaningful, worthwhile phase of human existence, which has its own character and its own value. This view is perhaps best expressed in Jacob Grimm's celebrated lecture of 1863, which was given to the Royal Academy of the Sciences in Berlin. Grimm said that while old age brings about a decline in vitality and physical strength, it also has a quality peculiar

---

[2] Cicero, *On Old Age*, trans. F. Copley (Ann Arbor: University of Michigan Press, 1967), pp. 37–38.

[3] See B. L. Richardson, *Old Age Among the Ancient Greeks* (Baltimore: Johns Hopkins, 1933).

[4] Lin Yutang, *The Wisdom of China and India* (New York: Modern Library, 1942), p. 814.

to itself that develops out of its own situation according to its own laws. "It is a time of peace and contentment which had not existed in the previous life and this condition therefore must also produce particular effects which correspond to this particular state."[5] This image of the aged person filled with wisdom and insight in which the tensions and stresses of earlier life have resolved themselves and given way to tranquillity and inner harmony is best exemplified by Goethe, who as an old man lived peacefully in Weimar, where he wrote the story of his life. It was there, shortly before his death at eighty-two, that he finished the second part of *Faust*, in which the hero, now an aged seer, finds the world so beautiful that he wishes it to remain as it is forever.

Modern psychologists have also stressed the fact that this final period is fundamentally different from the other stages of human life. While it is true that certain powers decline, there are others that develop so that old age has its redeeming features, some of which are unique. The Swiss psychologist Carl Jung expresses this idea in a very moving way:

Aging people should know that their lives are not mounting and unfolding, but that an inexorable inner process forces the contraction of life. . . . After having lavished its light upon the world, the sun withdraws its rays in order to illuminate itself. . . . A human being would certainly not grow to be seventy or eighty years old if this longevity had no meaning for the species to which he belongs. The afternoon of human life must also have a significance of its own and cannot be merely a pitiful appendage to life's morning. . . . Culture lies beyond the purposes of nature. Could by any chance culture be the meaning and purpose of the second half of life?[6]

Jung sees old age as a meaningful culmination of life, and he himself was a living example of this because he was active and cre-

---

[5] J. Grimm, *Rede Über das Alter*, reprint of 1863 edition, ed. H. Grimm (Kassel: Bärenreiter Verlag, 1963), pp. 69–70.
[6] C. J. Jung, *Modern Man in Search of a Soul* (New York: Harcourt Brace & World, 1933), p. 125.

ative right up to his death in 1961 at the age of eighty-six.

A very different view is held by other prominent writers, notably Simone de Beauvoir, who, in her celebrated book *The Coming of Age*, cites the British anthropologist Dr. Leach, who advocates scrapping all men over fifty-five like machines that have outlived their usefulness.[7] Another author she quotes is Jonathan Swift, who, although only fifty-five when he wrote about old age in *Gulliver's Travels*, produced what Beauvoir calls the cruelest portrait ever drawn. She says, "Old age, in so far as it was at least theoretically looked upon as the noblest, most perfected aspect of the human state, could not but arouse his fury. He was himself quite old; he was ill; and as it turned out his old age was in fact a disastrous physical and mental decay—it seemed that he had some premonition of it."[8]

Swift is certainly not the only one who has experienced old age as a purely negative phenomenon. In speaking of this stage, the Norwegian writer Knut Hamsun said that as he was growing old, he was growing old and nothing else. Probably the most savage and devastating of all portrayals are those in Beckett's plays *Endgame* and *Krapp's Last Tape*, where the author rages at the indignity and degradation of old age. The most famous depictions are found in Shakespeare's plays, although he never experienced these years, since he died in 1616 at fifty-two. His vision of the aged, demented Lear wandering about the heath is rightly considered one of his most profound psychological characterizations, and his comments on the last stages of man in *As You Like It* are justly famous.

> The sixth age shifts
> Into the lean and slippered Pantaloon
> With spectacles on nose and pouch on side,
> His youthful hose, well saved, a world too wide
> For his shrunk shank, and his big manly voice,
> Turning again toward childish treble, pipes
> And whistles in his sound. Last scene of all,

[7] Simone de Beauvoir, *The Coming of Age* (New York: G. P. Putnam's Sons, 1972), p. 15.
[8] Ibid, p. 281.

That ends this strange eventful history,
Is second childishness and mere oblivion,
Sans teeth, sans eyes, sans taste, sans everything.[9]

There is probably no gloomier assessment in literature of the close of our earthly existence.

In a statistical study, the psychologist Harvey Lehman[10] shows that most men of outstanding achievement produce their best work during their thirties, and that with forty a slow but steady decline begins. This is particularly true of scientists and mathematicians. Lehman gives the optimal age for superior creativity as twenty-six to thirty for chemists and thirty to thirty-five for physicists and mathematicians. An even earlier age is given for poets, who tend to reach their peak during their late twenties. According to Lehman, the best age for painters is between thirty-two and thirty-six, while that for sculptors is thirty-five to thirty-nine, and that for architects is forty to forty-four. However, it must be said that the data on which he bases his findings for the visual arts are grossly inadequate. For example, in sculpture he used only American artists instead of investigating a broad, well-selected sample of the many creative persons who have worked in this field.

A generation earlier, W. A. Newman Dorland undertook a similar study in which he tried to find out how age affected mental activity by studying the lives of some four hundred outstanding figures taken from a great variety of professions. His conclusions, based on fewer data than Professor Lehman's study employed and using a less scientific methodology, suggest that "the records give an average age of fifty for the performance of the master work."[11] He also found that virtually all those who performed on a superior level had already shown promise by the time they were twenty-five, and that, especially among composers and musicians, remarkable work

[9] William Shakespeare, *As You Like It*, Act II, Scene VII, lines 157–166.
[10] Harvey Lehman, *Age and Achievement* (Princeton: Princeton University Press, 1953).
[11] W. A. Newman Dorland, *The Age of Mental Virility: An Inquiry Into The Records of Achievement of the World's Chief Workers and Thinkers* (New York: The Century Co., 1908), p. 83.

had already been accomplished when they were still in their teens. Dorland also found that many men of genius exhibited a remarkable vitality and creative energy until late in life. Among the most exceptional was the scientist Michel Chevreul "whose untiring labors in the realm of color have enriched the world, who was busy, keen and active when death called him at the age of one hundred and three." Another example he gives is the German historian Leopold von Ranke, who began his *History of the World* at the age of eighty and completed ten volumes before he died at ninety-one, with his later work showing no decline despite the fact that he was still writing a few days before his death. Still another example is the German scholar Baron Alexander von Humboldt, who postponed until his seventy-sixth year what was to be the crowning work of his life, the preparation of *Kosmos*, a grand synthesis of the scientific knowledge of the universe. He successfully completed the work in his ninetieth year. Among writers the most noteworthy was probably Victor Hugo, who as a young man looked upon the aged poet as a prophet and seer, and who as an old man lived up to his vision by producing some of his finest work when he was in his seventies and eighties.

It would seem that most people reach the peak of their creativity relatively early in life, with their best work the product of their youth and early adulthood. However, there are others, including men of extraordinary genius like Michelangelo and Titian, who produced some of their finest work late in life. Many additional examples could be cited from other fields: Sophocles, who wrote *Oedipus Coloneus* when he was eighty-nine; Verdi, who produced some of his most outstanding operas during his seventies; and Beethoven, who wrote his late quartets at the very end of his life. In all these cases, old age, far from diminishing the creative power of the artists, seems to have deepened and strengthened it, giving their work a profundity and expressive quality that their early art did not possess.

German scholars use the word *Altersstil* to describe the phenomenon of the style that is a distinctive development of old age. It is characterized by a transcendent quality and a reduction of forms to their very essence. The late self-portraits of Rembrandt, the last works of Michelangelo, and the final phase of Donatello's oeuvre are usually regarded as the outstanding examples of this kind of old-age sensibility. In his lecture on artistic creativity in old age, Sir Kenneth Clark says,

> Now let me try to summarize the characteristics of old age style, as they appear with remarkable consistency, in the work of the greatest painters and sculptors. A sense of isolation, a feeling of holy rage, developing into what I have called transcendental pessimism, a mistrust of reason, a belief in instinct, and in a few instances the old age myth of classical antiquity—the feeling that the crimes and follies of mankind must be accepted with resignation. All this revealed by the imagery of old men's pictures, and to some extent by the treatment. If we consider old age art from a more narrowly stylistic point of view we find retreat from realism, an impatience with the established technique and a craving for complete unity of treatment as if the picture were an organism in which every member shares with reference to the whole.[12]

Interestingly enough, this kind of work, which today is so highly regarded, was misunderstood and often belittled by the artists' contemporaries. For example, Turner's late paintings, which modern critics consider the crowning achievement of his entire career, were not appreciated by most nineteenth-century art lovers, who saw them as the works of a madman in his artistic decline. Michelangelo's late frescoes in the Capella Paolina were considered cold and lifeless works that indicated deterioration of his creative power, and John Addington Symonds went so far as to lament the fact that the artist used up seven years to produce them. It is very much a twentieth-century judgment that prefers Michelangelo's late *Pietà* in Florence, with its abstract and expressive forms, to his early *Pietà* in Rome, which other periods had considered vastly superior. Monet's late paintings provide another example of this change in judgment, for during his own lifetime they were almost completely ignored, but today they are considered among his very finest work.

It must be said at once that this kind of ultimate revelation

---

[12] Kenneth Clark, *The Artist Grows Old* (Cambridge: Cambridge University Press, 1972), pp. 21–22.

during the late years of life is extremely rare. Far more common are the artists who live to an advanced age but suffer a serious decline, Picasso being perhaps the outstanding example of such. Although he reached his nineties, he had stopped creating any significant work long before his death. Also rare are the artists who continue throughout their old age to produce at the same level of excellence with undiminished vigor. One example is Matisse, who, although crippled in his last years, made paper cutouts that today are ranked among his most remarkable creations. Even more exceptional are the artists who emerge as major figures in their old age after years of rather ordinary work, not to mention those who take up an artistic career in old age, having spent most of their lives in some other profession. Most of the last mentioned usually become amateurs or primitives because they have never received any formal training. The only exceptions are the Chinese and Japanese gentlemen scholar-artists who had studied painting and calligraphy as part of their regular education and, after retirement, took up artistic careers.

All these observations are, of course, based upon artists who actually reached old age, men who lived to their seventies or eighties, and in some cases even nineties, who led an active creative life that extended well beyond the life expectancy of the average person. Many others lived to a ripe old age but were incapacitated by various infirmities, such as the blindness that prevented Piero della Francesca from painting in his last years. Still others were cut short by an early death, such as Masaccio, who died in his twenties, and Caravaggio, who was killed in a brawl at thirty-seven. One can only speculate on the magnificent work they might have produced had they lived into old age. Who knows what the history of English landscape painting would have been if Thomas Girtin, whom Turner regarded as his only peer, had not died at twenty-six but had lived to his seventies or eighties? One feels certain that Franz Marc, who perished in the First World War at thirty-six, and Paula Modersohn-Becker, who died in childbirth at thirty-one, would have played a far more important role in modern German art if they had lived out a full life. Unfortunately, we will never be able to see the *Altersstil* of Raphael and innumerable others who, although possessing great gifts, even genius, never had the opportunity to develop an old-age style.

# A DISTINCT STYLE IN OLD AGE

$O$f all the artists who had a true *Altersstil*, by far the most outstanding was Michelangelo. The last thirty years of his life, from 1534, when at the age of fifty-nine he settled permanently in Rome, to 1564, the time of his death at the age of eighty-nine, was a period of unsurpassed creativity during which he worked in a style that is very different from the one he employed in his earlier years. Our leading Michelangelo scholar, Charles de Tolnay, characterizes these years in the following words: "They constitute a distinct phase in the spiritual and artistic development of the master. Recently it has been emphasized that this period was not an epoch of decadence but rather of a change in Michelangelo's conceptions and in his artistic language. Also there was a shift from the figurative arts of sculpture and painting to the abstract art of architecture and poetry."[1] It was during this period that Michelangelo produced some of his greatest works. Under the

[1] Charles de Tolnay, *Michelangelo*, vol. 5, *The Final Period* (Princeton: Princeton University Press, 1960), Introduction.

patronage of the Farnese Pope Paul III, who ruled for the first fifteen of these thirty years, the artist received some of his most important commissions. In 1535, when Michelangelo was sixty years old, the Pope declared him to be the world's foremost sculptor, painter, and architect, put him in charge of the arts of the Vatican at a lifetime income of twelve hundred gold ducats a year, and treated him as an equal, with all the respect and consideration a man of such genius deserved. At the same time, this was also a period of growing religious preoccupation in which Michelangelo's thoughts turned increasingly toward God and the salvation of his soul. His personal life was also a very rich one, surrounded as he was by a circle of devoted friends and admirers. Among the most important were Vittoria Colonna, whom he befriended when he was sixty-three and she forty-six and with whom he had a purely Platonic relationship; the beautiful youth Tommaso de Cavalieri, with whom he fell in love when he was fifty-eight and entered a lasting friendship; and Giorgio Vasari, who became not only a good friend but his chronicler in the celebrated *Lives of the Painters, Sculptors, and Architects.*

Yet in spite of all this, Michelangelo's old age was a period of physical infirmity, frustration, and anxiety over the fate of his soul. As early as 1516 to 1518, when he was a man in his early forties, he was already talking about himself as an old man, and forty-eight years before the actual event he was writing about his imminent death in one of his poems.[2] In 1547, when he was seventy-two, he wrote in a letter to his friend Martini, "I bear with patience the sufferings of old age," and in 1550, when he was seventy-five and had fourteen more years to live, "I wrestle with Death," and to Vasari in 1555, "There exists no thought within which Death is not sculpted."[3] At another time he said: "I am old, and death has stolen from me the ideas of my youth, and he who does not know what old age is should wait with patience until it arrives, since before that he cannot know what it is."[4] There can be no doubt that he did suffer

[2] Robert J. Clements, *Michelangelo—A Self Portrait* (New York: New York University Press, 1968), p. 168.
[3] Ibid.
[4] Tolnay, *Michelangelo*, p. 14.

from all kinds of infirmities. He had trouble with kidney stones, for which he had been treated by a physician; he suffered a fall; and he complained of his inability to sleep. Yet in a discussion of his health, Vasari, who knew him well and was in constant contact with him, says, "He remained healthy until his ninetieth year, in full enjoyment of his faculties and so strong that he worked up to the very last day."[5] Michelangelo himself, speaking of his working habits, said, "I try harder than any man there ever was, ill in health and with greatest effort. And yet I have patience to get the desired end." At another time he said, "I enjoy and thrive on precisely what kills others." What kept him going was his love for his work, to which he devoted his entire life with single-minded obsession, and his abiding faith, which in spite of all doubt and anguish made him, when he made his last will, "leave his soul to God, his body to the earth and his property to his nearest relations," warning his friends in this passing life to remember the Passion of Christ; and so, as Vasari relates, he passed to a better life.[6]

The first major work of Michelangelo's late period was *The Last Judgment*, which was originally commissioned by Pope Clement VII but was actually painted under Paul III in the Sistine Chapel of the Vatican in which he had painted his famous ceiling a generation earlier. Begun in 1535, when the artist was sixty, the work occupied him for six years, two years longer than the ceiling. The finished work was unveiled on Christmas Day in 1541, when he was sixty-six years old, and aroused the admiration of the world. The Pope himself is said to have fallen down on his knees in prayer and adoration in front of this masterpiece, and artists from all over Italy flocked to the chapel to see this divine work. Vasari felt that this sublime painting should serve as a model for all art and thought that even "the most learned craftsman will tremble when he sees those bold outlines and those marvelous foreshortenings." Romain Rolland, in his life of Michelangelo, has this to say about the picture: "It was the work of an old man between sixty and sixty-five; the vitality which this terrible old man still possessed after a life of

[5] Hinds, translator, and W. Gaunt, editor, *Lives of the Painters, Sculptors and Architects*, vol. 4 (London: Everyman's Library, 1970), p. 182.
[6] Ibid., p. 170.

exhausting labours and troubles, whatever we may think of the work, is something superhuman. . . . Men came from all over Italy and from abroad to be present at its unveiling on December 25, 1541. Hosts of Italian, French, Flemish and German artists followed each other without respite through the Sistine Chapel, copying zealously the entire fresco, and the glory of Michelangelo far from being diminished, as Aretino predicted, became colossal on account of it."[7] A huge fresco, measuring forty-eight by forty-four feet, it covered the entire wall above the altar and included over one hundred large nude figures shown in violent motion. Presiding over them is the monumental figure of Christ, who on the day of Last Judgment is seen judging mankind. In contrast to the ceiling with its serene and harmonious High Renaissance forms, the figures in this fresco show the distortion and exaggeration characteristic of Mannerism and reveal the aged artist in a completely new phase of his artistic and spiritual development.

A few months later Michelangelo began another major work for the Pope: the fresco *Conversion of St. Paul* for the Pauline Chapel in the Vatican, which was to occupy him from 1542 to 1545, that is, from his sixty-seventh to his seventieth year. This was followed by a second fresco for the same chapel, *Crucifixion of St. Peter.* It occupied him, along with other projects, from 1546 to 1550, so that he was seventy-five when both pictures were completed. It is said that Michelangelo, in representing the conversion of Paul, not only was portraying the historical event itself but was also making reference to his own conversion, reflecting the deep religious feeling of his old age and the spirit of the Counter Reformation, which was taking place at that time. These frescoes, which were his last paintings, have traditionally not been very highly regarded, and many critics who praised the pictures in the Sistine Chapel have seen in these works nothing but the decline and the lessening of creative power on the part of the aging artist. In fact, they have suffered from neglect and few visitors to the Vatican even today take the trouble to look at these masterpieces of Michelangelo's late period. It has only been in recent years that modern critics, approaching them

[7] Romain Rolland, *Michelangelo* (New York: Boni & Liveright, 1915), p. 92 and p. 101.

with very different artistic criteria from their predecessors', have rediscovered them and placed them in their proper context as important contributions to the development of sixteenth-century Italian painting. It may also have helped that the frescoes have been cleaned and restored, bringing out even more the extraordinary beauty of their colors. The most recent and perceptive study devoted to them is by Leo Steinberg, who, after saying that they have been misunderstood and neglected for centuries, comments, "To reinstitute these works in the corpus of valid artistic expression required new lines of approach. Some proceeded from the supposed psychology of old age; some by assimilating them to the stylistic definition of Mannerism; others, through a felt affinity with contemporary art forms—Expressionism and Abstraction—converting Michelangelo's last frescoes into figurative equivalents of modern paintings, essentially abstract and secular."[8] The result was a complete reassessment of their artistic worth and a proper placement of them in the artist's entire oeuvre.

Of the sculptures of Michelangelo's old age, by far the most outstanding are the two *Pietàs*, one intended for his own tomb and executed intermittently between 1550 and 1555, between his seventy-fifth and eightieth years, and the other, the last work with which he was still engaged at the time of his death, begun when he was already eighty years old. The choice of this subject matter was not pure chance, for between 1550 and 1555 the artist made numerous drawings of subjects such as the Lamentation, the Crucifixion, and the Entombment, indicating his preoccupation with the suffering and death of Christ. It is also characteristic of his state of mind at this stage of his life that he should have included a self-portrait in the form of Joseph of Arimathaea (referred to as Nicodemus by Vasari), reflecting his very personal feeling about this event. This sculpture, which he never finished, was given by Michelangelo to his servant Antonio del Francesa, who had prevented the artist from destroying it in a fit of rage. After the master's death it was completed by his pupil Tiberio Calgani, who patched the smashed arms and finished the Mary Magdalene. It was acquired by

[8] Leo Steinberg, *Michelangelo's Last Paintings* (New York: Oxford University Press, 1975), p. 20.

Michelangelo Buonarroti
Pietà
*1500*
St. Peter's, Rome

Michelangelo executed this early
masterpiece, the Pietà, when he was
twenty-five years old.

Michelangelo Buonarroti
Pietà *or* Deposition
*1550–1555*
Santa Maria Del Fiore, Florence

This deeply moving Pietà, one of only
two sculptures Michelangelo executed
during the last twenty years of his life,
was intended for his tomb. He was
eighty when in 1555 the work was
completed.

the Medici Grand Duke Cosimo III for the city of Florence and was placed first in the crypt of San Lorenzo and finally in the cathedral, where it is now in the chapel of the north transept. Critics have rightly considered it one of the most moving and profound of all the artist's works. Frederick Hartt, in his recent book on Michelangelo's *Pietàs*, calls his depiction of Christ's sinking body "one of the most compelling, even irresistible movements in all of man's artistic expression."[9] Compared to the sensuously beautiful classical forms of the artist's early *Pietà* of fifty years earlier in St. Peter's, his treatment of the sacred figures here has a simplicity and strength that is remarkable indeed and brings to this theme a kind of religious emotion that is deeply felt and expresses the artist's own preoccupation with suffering, death, and redemption, questions that he was profoundly concerned with during the last years of his life.

Even more striking is his very last sculpture, known today as the Rondanini *Pietà*, named after the Palazzo Rondanini in Rome, where it was on display for many years. However, in 1952 it was acquired by the city of Milan, where it is today in the Castello Sforzesco. The creation of this group, comprising only Mary and Christ, has a very long and complicated history. Scholars studying the matter distinguish, on the basis of drawings and reports, between a first stage from after 1552 and second and third stages dating from between late 1563 and the time of Michelangelo's death in 1564. Vasari reports that he was still working on the statue shortly before his death, and it is certainly his last and most transcendental artistic statement. It is reported that in order to complete the work he made a paper cap for himself to which he attached a candle so that he could work at night when he suffered from insomnia. Yet the sculpture remained unfinished. Hartt refers to it as a final testament of the artist, while Tolnay says "that from a certain point of view it represents the culmination of his art."[10] Again they reflect the contemporary critical view, which tends to prefer incomplete works to highly finished ones and more abstract and simple forms to more naturalistic and detailed ones. Nevertheless, there can be no doubt that we have here an ultimate statement on the part of the aged

[9] Frederick Hartt, *Michelangelo's Three Pietàs* (New York: Abrams, 1975), p. 82.
[10] Tolnay, *Michelangelo*, p. 10.

genius similar to Beethoven's late quartets or Shakespeare's last plays, in which the aged artist transcends artistic conventions and gives expression to his most profound and personal sentiments. Tolnay very rightly called these late works of Michelangelo "like confessions or lonely prayers."[11] Since sixteenth-century taste, however, demanded that a sculpture be finished, it was no doubt at the time considered an incomplete work produced largely for the artist's own satisfaction, as were many of the late drawings. Yet these final statements of the aged Michelangelo, now in his ninetieth year, are among the greatest and most expressive works of his artistic career.

The most ambitious project of Michelangelo's entire life, and the most important work of his old age, was the design for a new St. Peter's. He was appointed to the position of chief architect for the building by Pope Paul III after the death of Antonio de Sangallo the Younger in 1546. Although he was not really an architect by training and had initially turned down this assignment, he reluctantly accepted it at the command of the Pope and served in this capacity until the time of his death some two decades later. He did so, as he himself said, "solely for the love of God and out of reverence for the Prince of the Apostles." Although he was seventy-one at the time, he embarked upon this task with the enthusiasm and energy of a man half his age, and at eighty-five could still be seen inspecting the construction at St. Peter's on horseback. In 1563, at the age of eighty-eight, the building commission, under the influence of Nanni de Baccio Bigio, tried to have him removed. Michelangelo appealed to the Pope to permit him to continue the work he had begun. Pope Pius IV, who at that time occupied the papal throne, confirmed him in his position and granted him greater powers than those enjoyed by any of the previous architects who had been engaged in this project.

The plan for this magnificent structure, which was to become the most famous of all Christian churches, had had a long and complicated history going back to the time of Bramante, to whose basic Greek cross design Michelangelo returned. In 1546 he first made a small clay model of the building, which was followed by a larger

[11] Ibid.

wooden one made the next year, and by several later models for the drum and the dome, which was to dominate the entire church. Although the cathedral was not completed as he had envisaged it, for the outer shell of the dome was reworked by Giacomo della Porta and the entire western side of the building was changed completely by Maderna, much of the basic conception, with its central plan, colossal orders, and great dome, was executed the way he had planned it. At the time of his death the construction had only progressed to the drum of the dome, but enough had been completed of this huge building so that the later architects had to follow his general ideas, with the exception of the façade, which was completely changed.

While the construction of this great edifice over the remains of St. Peter was no doubt his most significant work as an architect, there were several other building projects of note that he supervised or in which he played an important role. Notable among them are the plans for the Capitoline Hill, the center of ancient Rome, for which he designed the Palazzo Senatorio with its grand outside stairway. He was also involved in the reconstruction of the fortifications of Rome and the completion of the Farnese Palace, for which he designed the upper story and cornice, and he prepared plans for a number of other building projects such as the Church of San Giovanni dei Fiorentini in Rome, the staircase for the Biblioteca Laurenziana in Florence, and the transformation of the thermae of Diocletian into Santa Maria degli Angeli. While all the works were, of course, executed by others after his drawings and ideas, they nevertheless indicate how vigorous and active Michelangelo was when he was already in his eighties.

Michelangelo continued his artistic activity up to the day of his death on February 18, 1564. We are told in a letter by Daniele da Volterra to his nephew Lionardo that he was at work on his last *Pietà* as late as five days before his death. His passing was marked by one of the grandest funerals ever held in Florence. Noted artists such as Bronzino, Vasari, Cellini, and Ammanati made the arrangements, and all of Florence came to San Lorenzo to witness the last rites performed for its greatest native son. In a letter to the Duke of Florence, the vice-president of the Academy and Company of Painters and Sculptors referred to Michelangelo as "the greatest artist of their profession, who had perhaps ever lived." Thus ended an artistic career that spanned over seventy years. This extraordinary genius, probably the greatest artist the Western world has produced, created some of the masterpieces of world art in the fields of sculpture, painting, and architecture, several of the finest of these during the last three decades of his life.

Another great High Renaissance artist who had a distinct old-age style was Michelangelo's contemporary Titian. It was long believed that Titian was born in 1477, which would have made him ninety-nine at the time of his death and would have meant that he produced some of his greatest paintings when he was already in his nineties. However, modern scholarship has ascertained that he was actually born in 1488, so he lived to be only eighty-eight. His late period is usually dated from the 1540s, beginning perhaps during his visit to Rome in 1545. There he met the aged Michelangelo and painted the portrait of Pope Paul III and his grandsons, a picture now in Naples and considered one of his masterpieces. This late style of the artist is marked by a new sense of drama, looser brushwork, and, above all, a softer and more brilliant use of color, which becomes the main medium of artistic expression. It is a style very different from that of Michelangelo, who, even when painting, remained very much a sculptor interested primarily in form and line. It is not surprising that, according to Vasari, while Michelangelo admired the work of Titian, he chided him for not having studied drawing sufficiently. It is, of course, precisely this magnificent use of color that makes Titian's work in general, and especially his late work, so memorable. In fact, it is during this late period that the artist painted some of his finest pictures. As Frederick Hartt put it, "The great master burst out again with renewed and surprising heat in an uninterrupted series of passionate works, from the early 1540s until the aged painter was stopped by death." He adds, "History holds few examples of such regeneration."[12]

In the 1540s Titian was a man in his fifties and was to enjoy

[12] Frederick Hartt, *History of Italian Renaissance Art* (New York: Prentice-Hall, 1969), p. 541.

another thirty years of unbroken artistic creativity that was in no way inferior to the work of his youth or middle age. In these late paintings the solid forms dissolve more and more into light and color, and his interpretation of human nature becomes ever more profound. Finally, there is in this art, as there had been in the late work of Michelangelo, a turning toward Christianity, with an increased emphasis on themes such as the Crowning with Thorns, Entombment, and Lamentation, depicted with a religious fervor absent in his earlier work. Be it that the aged Titian personally became more devout as he neared the end of his life, as is often the case with old people, or that the spirit of the Counter Reformation had affected him, there is no doubt that not only the style but also the subject matter of the paintings of his old age exhibit very distinct characteristics not found in his earlier work.

Unlike Michelangelo, who suffered from many ailments, Titian remained in excellent health right into his eighties and enjoyed a rich and pleasurable life. Vasari, who visited him in 1566, found him vigorous and occupied with painting at his home, working for pleasure and at the request of princes and friends. He further reports that "His house in Venice has been frequented by all the princes, learned men and gallants of the time, because in addition to his genius he possesses the most courtly manners. He has had some rivals in Venice whom he has easily surpassed, and he has retained the favor of nobles. He gained much wealth as his pictures have been well paid for, and in his later years he would have done well to have worked only for amusement, in order not to circulate works which may damage a reputation won in his best years."[13]

Blessed with favorable circumstances, for as Vasari said, Titian was always "a most healthy and fortunate man, beyond any of his fellows, and received nothing but favors from Heaven," Titian continued to pour out a wealth of masterpieces to the very day of his death, at which time he, like Michelangelo, was creating a *Pietà* in which he introduced himself in the guise of Joseph of Arimathaea kneeling in front of the dead Savior. This work, now in the Accademia in Venice, had originally been intended for his tomb.

Many of the finest canvases of Titian's old age represent reli-

---

[13] Hinds and Gaunt, *Lives*, p. 211.

gious subjects, such as the moving *Entombment* in Madrid and the dramatic *Christ Crowned with Thorns* in Munich. While he brings to these themes a heightened sense of religious drama anticipating the Baroque, he also painted a great many secular subjects largely taken from Greek mythology. His famous *Danae* in Naples embodies the very essence of the glorification of sensuous beauty with its soft treatment of flesh and vibrant colors exhibiting the Venetian style of painting at its best. Even more impressive is the far more ambitious *Rape of Europa* in the Isabella Stewart Gardner Museum in Boston. It is believed to have been painted in 1560, when the artist was seventy-two years old. In it all the characteristics

*Titian*
The Rape of Europa
*1560*
*Courtesy Isabella Stewart Gardner Museum, Boston*

*Titian's artistry was at its peak in 1560, as is demonstrated by his painting* The Rape of Europa, *completed when the master was seventy-two years old.*

of his old-age style can be seen at their best, with shimmering, pulsating color applied in free, loose strokes, and a divine eroticism surpassing even that of his earlier work.

Magnificent, too, are Titian's old-age portraits, notably those of Charles V, with whom he maintained very cordial relations. These portraits are among his most profound and penetrating interpretations of human nature. Other pictures in this genre show his daughter Lavinia, whose beauty he celebrated in several canvases. Most moving of all are the self-portraits of his old age, especially the magnificent picture, dated 1562, in the Prado in Madrid, which depicts the artist in his seventy-fourth year. In this portrait Titian shows us the master as a man of serene old age, self-possessed and conscious of his dignity and physical beauty as well as his exalted position among his fellowmen. The equal of emperors and Popes, he holds his paintbrush in his hand, indicating that he, the aged Titian, is a person of genius who need bow to no man alive. He died of pestilence in 1576 at the age of eighty-eight, and his funeral was celebrated by the citizens of Venice with the same pomp accorded Michelangelo by the Florentines a decade earlier.

The third great Italian Renaissance artist who had a definite old-age style was Donatello, who lived from 1386 to 1466. In fact, it was to his work that the term *Altersstil* was first applied. Here again many of the features that had marked the late work of Michelangelo and Titian may be observed. An increase of dramatic feeling, a more abstract treatment of the forms, and, above all, a greater depth of religious feeling, which no doubt reflected the very different climate of opinion that prevailed in Florence during the 1450s and reached its culmination in the period when Savonarola was at the height of his influence. Frederick Hartt, speaking of the late sculptures, characterizes them in the following words: "These late works of Donatello admit us to a hitherto unexplored inner world of emotional stress, and study with fascination the ravages of time and decay and the human body whose youthful beauty a happier generation had discovered with joy."[14]

14 Hartt, *History*, p. 250.

This phase of the artist's career starts in 1453, when he was sixty-three years old, with his return to Florence from Padua, where he had spent nearly a decade. It ends with his death at the age of eighty, thirteen years later. While this style is already anticipated in certain statues done when Donatello was in his early fifties, such as the John the Baptist he made for the Frari Church in Venice, it only appears in its fully developed form in his Mary Magdalene, executed for the Baptistry in Florence in 1456, in his John the Baptist in the cathedral in Siena, and above all, in his masterpiece of this period, the *Judith and Holofernes*, which was acquired by the Medici and is now in the Piazza della Signoria in Florence. It is in these works of his old age that we see the master, who was already a man of seventy, at the height of his creative power.

Vasari, who visited him as an old man, reported that Donatello spent his old age happily and that Cosimo de Medici himself saw to it that he was well taken care of by settling an annual income on him. His leading position in the Florentine art scene as the undisputed master of Quattrocento sculpture, surrounded by devoted pupils and able assistants, was generally acknowledged, for as Vasari said, "Donatello single handed brought perfection and delight back to our age by the multitude of his works. . . . Thus artists ought to recognize the greatness of his art more than of any modern, for he, besides rendering the difficulties of art easy by the number of his works, united in himself that invention, design, skill, judgement and every other faculty that can or ought to be expected in a man of genius."[15] Far from showing a decline in his later years, the artist continued to be very productive into his old age and stopped working only after becoming sick at the very end of his life when he was almost eighty years old.

The last important commissions of his career, which in fact he was not able to complete himself, were the two pulpits for the Church of San Lorenzo in Florence, where he was buried near his great patron Cosimo the Elder. Begun in 1460 and completed by his assistants around 1470, four years after his death, these last works are among the most moving of all Renaissance sculptures. The themes represented are characteristic of his preoccupation with death

[15] Hinds and Gaunt, *Lives*, p. 313.

*Donatello*
Lamentation
*c. 1450*
*Courtesy Victoria and Albert Museum, London*

*It is believed that Donatello executed the* Lamentation *in 1450, during his*
*sixty-fourth year.*

and suffering, dwelling upon the Passion of Christ and culminating
in the Crucifixion, Deposition, and Resurrection. Other scenes depict
the martyrdom of Lawrence, the patron saint of the church and the
Medici family. The style of these sculptures from the last phase of
Donatello's art has been described as coarse by a sixteenth-century
critic[16] for it no longer conformed to the classical ideals of the
earlier Renaissance. However, during the twentieth century it has
been particularly admired for its expressive quality, which is much
closer to modern art in its distortion of form and intensity of emotion than it is to the humanistic naturalism of his earlier works.

Of the seventeenth-century artists who had a distinct old-age style, it
is Rembrandt who is the most outstanding. Although he actually did
not live to be very old, for he died at the age of sixty-three in 1669,

[16] H. W. Janson: *The Sculpture of Donatello*, vol. 2 (Princeton: Princeton University
Press, 1957), p. 209.

he developed a true *Altersstil* during the last years of his life, at which time he painted some of his most profound and moving pictures. Bob Haak, in his monumental book on the life and work of Rembrandt,[17] divides the master's artistic career into five major periods, the last of which, according to him, starts in 1662 and comprises the last seven years of his life. He describes this last phase in the following words:

> The remaining years were characterized by a strongly diminishing productivity. Rembrandt had virtually ceased to etch and also made fewer drawings. But in painting he showed no decline, had indeed not yet reached the peak. His palette became richer and more subtle than ever before: warm reds, bronze, greens, ochres combined with white and deep black to form an enchanting play of colors, accentuated by the techniques he used to build up the impasto, employing both brush and palette knife. These techniques deviated vigorously from the classical conception being followed by other artists, who painted in a smooth, glossy style. At last Rembrandt's art reached its ultimate perfection in the one picture which I place at the very pinnacle of his art: *The Bridal Couple.*

While the choice of *The Bridal Couple*, also often referred to as *The Jewish Bride* and believed to have been painted in 1665, seems to be rather arbitrary and reflects a judgment few other critics would share, there is general agreement that it was during these last years of Rembrandt's life that the aged artist produced some of his finest work. The beginning of this *Altersstil* can be dated to the largest and most ambitious painting of Rembrandt's old age, the *Conspiracy of Claudius Civilis*, now in the National Museum in Stockholm, Sweden. It was originally commissioned by the city of Amsterdam for the new town hall and was completed in 1662, when the painter was fifty-six years old. It was a huge painting, measuring 550 centimeters square, but after being removed from its original location because the artist had refused to make certain changes the

[17] B. Haak, *Rembrandt, His Life, His Work, His Time* (New York: Abrams, 1969), p. 334.

city had requested, it was cut down in size to 196 centimeters by 309 centimeters and turned over to an art dealer. The subject depicted is taken from Tacitus and deals with the conspiracy of the Batavians, the ancestors of the Dutch, who under one of their chieftains, Claudius Civilis, conspired against the Romans, their oppressors. Painted in a very loose style with magnificent yellows, reds, and browns, it is one of the master's most impressive pictures in which his use of chiaroscuro and inspired brushwork can be seen at its best. In this late work Rembrandt's style has become more and more abstract and suggestive, dissolving matter into a pattern of light and color, completely transcending the realism of his earlier work.

A slightly later picture from the same period is his last major official commission, *The Syndics of the Cloth Guild*, now in the Rijksmuseum in Amsterdam. This group portrait, which was also painted in 1662, is rightly regarded as one of Rembrandt's masterpieces and one of the outstanding pictures of an artistic genre that enjoyed great popularity in seventeenth-century Holland. Surpassing even *The Anatomy Lesson* and *The Night Watch* of his earlier years, the painting gives a penetrating characterization of the various types of men assembled and shows the painter's mastery in the use of blacks and whites against the deep reds and browns of the setting. There can be no doubt that Rembrandt, far from declining as he reached his old age, achieved a depth of expression and a beauty of color and design greater than he had known before.

Numerous other paintings from the final years of the artist's life could be mentioned, every one of them a masterpiece, for while his output may have decreased in quantity and fewer commissions came to the increasingly reclusive artist, the quality of his work reached a height never achieved in his earlier years. In the realm of portraiture, especially the self-portraits, such as the magnificent likenesss of the aged Rembrandt in the Wallraf-Richartz Museum in Cologne, painted in 1668, or the portraits of friends and unknown sitters such as the *Family Group*, now in the Herzog Anton Ulrich Museum in Brunswick, with its depiction of human tenderness and its use of yellows and reds against the darker background, his late work is unsurpassed.

Other subjects treated are taken from Greek mythology and

Roman history, excellent examples of which are the *Juno*, now on loan at The Metropolitan Museum of Art, and the dramatic *Lucretia* of 1664 in the National Gallery in Washington. However, at least in the eyes of this writer, the greatest of all these pictures done in his old age and perhaps the finest religious painting of his entire career is his rendering of the New Testament story of the Prodigal Son. Worked on from 1668 to 1669, the year of his death, it is now in the Hermitage in Leningrad. This final work combines all those qualities that make Rembrandt such a great and profound artist— the depth of religious feeling, the beautiful use of dark and light, the marvelous command of his medium, and the ability to say so much with such an economy of means. There is no doubt that the artist, who at this time was in his sixties and on the threshold of death, brings to this theme a profound emotion and deeply felt humanity that surpass anything he had been capable of during the earlier periods of his life. Having experienced sufferings and losses himself in the death of his son Titus and his wife Hendrickje, he brings to this story a compassion and emotional rapport that is found only in the work of his old age.

Nineteenth-century critics put a great emphasis upon the pov-

*Rembrandt van Rijn*
Lucretia
*1664*
*Courtesy National Gallery of Art,*
*Andrew W. Mellon Collection,*
*Washington, D.C.*

*One of Rembrandt's finest*
*historical portraits, the dramatic*
Lucretia, *was painted in 1664,*
*the artist's fifty-ninth year.*

erty and neglect of Rembrandt during his old age, since it confirmed their romantic view of the artist as a lonely outsider. However, modern critics such as Seymour Slive[18] have come to the conclusion that this picture is overdrawn. Although he probably had no pupils during the very last years of his life, as late as 1661 Aert de Gelder studied under him, as had such prominent artists as Dou, Bol, Fabritius, Maes, and the well-known English painter Godfrey Kneller. Commissions, especially for portraits, were given to him by such prominent persons as the Grand Duke of Tuscany, Cosimo III, who visited Rembrandt in his studio in 1667 and bought one of his self-portraits, which was much admired in Florence. He continued to enjoy a great reputation not only in his native Holland but in Flanders, Italy, England, and Germany. An Italian critic, Abate Filippo Baldinucci, wrote the first full-length account of the artist's life and work in his book on the art of engraving and etching. The Italian collector Don Antonio Ruffo not only commissioned a painting of the blind Homer from him but preferred his late pictures to those of his early period and in 1669, the year of the artist's death, ordered and received 189 Rembrandt etchings.

It is true that he was forced to declare bankruptcy in 1656, but this was due more to extravagance and to poor management of his financial affairs than to actual poverty, and it did not affect his creative life. In fact, it may be said that the inwardness and profundity of his last pictures are related to his withdrawal from the world, for as Otto Benesch said, "The great Rembrandt is above all the later Rembrandt. . . . There can be no doubt that this art, expressing everything in an elemental language of color, had a special significance for Rembrandt."[19] As with Michelangelo and Titian, his late paintings reveal the very essence of the human experience and give expression to the ultimate spiritual reality.

The two other great Baroque painters who had a distinct old-age style were El Greco and Frans Hals. El Greco, or to use his true name, Domenikos Theotokopoulos, was born on the island of Crete

---

[18] Seymour Slive, *Rembrandt and His Critics* (The Hague: M. Nijhof, 1953).
[19] Otto Benesch, *Rembrandt*, translated by J. Emmons (Cleveland: Skira, 1957), p. 81.

in 1541 and died in Toledo, Spain, in 1614 at the age of seventy-three. His life's work is usually divided into the three periods. The early one, when he was under the influence of the Venetian masters and the Mannerists, lasted from about 1558 to 1577, the year he went to Spain. This was followed by his artistic maturity during the 1580s and 1590s when he developed his characteristic style and produced such masterpieces as *The Burial of the Count of Orgaz*, which was completed in 1586, and a late period, which started around 1600, his sixtieth year, and lasted until his death. While the change in his style is less dramatic than the transformation that occurred in Rembrandt's work and less distinctive than that in the old-age work of Michelangelo, there is nevertheless a new intensity in his late pictures that sets them apart. At least one scholar has written an entire book devoted to the paintings of his final years, pointing out that in them one finds a distinctive manner that had already been commented upon by nineteenth-century critics.[20]

The style of these late works has often been described as Expressionistic, and it is not pure chance that these pictures, which at one point were thought to have been the result of an eye defect, have had a special appeal to the artists and critics of the twentieth century. Like the modern artist, El Greco in these paintings of his old age has taken great liberties with natural forms, distorting and changing them arbitrarily, so that they sometimes look like white flames seen against a dramatically illuminated landscape setting. The colors themselves are strange. Vivid greens, bright orange-reds, brilliant lemon yellows, and deep blues are used in a very effective way, producing often dissonant but very expressive color combinations that are aesthetically pleasing.

However, it is not so much the formal devices but the spirit of these pictures that makes them so memorable. Their religious intensity, bordering on spiritual frenzy, is truly remarkable, producing a pictorial equivalent of the ecstatic visions of St. John of the Cross and St. Theresa of Avila. In them the ardor of the Catholic faith of the Counter Reformation finds its most fervent expression, and Harold Wethey is not far off when he says that in these works, "El Greco

---

[20] E. Lafuente Ferrari, *El Greco, the Expressionism of His Final Years* (New York: Abrams, 1969).

*El Greco*
Opening of the Fifth Seal
*1610–1614*
*Courtesy The Metropolitan*
*Museum of Art,*
*Rogers Fund, 1956,*
*New York*

*El Greco painted* Opening of
the Fifth Seal, *one of his*
*finest late works, between*
*1610 and 1614—his*
*sixty-ninth to seventy-third*
*years.*

was able to achieve a greater intensity than any other master in the long history of painting."[21]

Many fine pictures were painted during the last period of the artist's life, such as the numerous versions of the Adoration of the Shepherds, the Crucifixion, and the Resurrection, as well as the portraits of Fra Hortensio Paravicino and Cardinal Guevara and the magnificent *View of Toledo* in The Metropolitan Museum of Art in New York. However, there are two paintings of his old age that stand out above the rest, and they are the *Opening of the Fifth Seal* and the *Laocoön*. The former picture, which was painted between 1610 and 1614, used to be in the collection of the Spanish painter Zuloaga but is now in The Metropolitan Museum of Art, while the depiction of the Laocoön myth is in the National Gallery in Washington. We see in them the final culmination of El Greco's old-age

---

[21] Harold E. Wethey, *El Greco and His School* (Princeton: Princeton University Press, 1962), p. 482.

style. Here he transcends the natural world and gives us a dreamlike vision of a realm of spiritual essences in which matter dissolves into pure light and color. The forms lose all mass and weight and float in a space that is far removed from the world of our everyday experience. The bodies of the figures are elongated to a point where they no longer seem real but become part of some new spiritual world that represents El Greco's ultimate revelation.

No documentary evidence has been found for the exact date of Frans Hals's birth, but it is believed that he was born in Antwerp between 1581 and 1585, with the latter the preferred date. This would mean that he was in his early eighties when he died in 1666. His late period, during which he developed a distinct old-age style, started in 1650, when he was probably sixty-five, and continued to the time of his death. Here again, as in the case of El Greco, the works of his old age used to be thought of as indicating the decline of his creative power. The famous German art historian Wilhelm von Bode spoke of an infirmity of brushwork resulting from his hands' trembling as he painted these late canvases, while Reynolds and Goethe thought of them as being unfinished. Contemporary scholars and critics, however, see these pictures of his late years as the culmination of his life's work and think of the very qualities that were once considered the result of decrepitude as the hallmark of his genius. Seymour Slive, in his study of the great Dutch painter, put it this way: "Hals did not get bored with portrait painting. On the contrary, his most persuasive characterizations were made during his last phase, when he convinces us that he has probed deeply into the personalities of the burghers and the meek, the brutal and the tender. Frontal poses became more frequent and in his pictures this stock attitude always gives us a startling sense of the presence of a fellow human being."[22]

The style of his old age, like that of Titian, became ever freer, the brushwork looser, and the forms simpler, at the same time revealing a depth of psychological insight that is remarkable indeed. While his earlier portraits dwelt mainly on the outward appearance

[22] Seymour Slive, *Frans Hals*, vol. 1 (London: Phaidon, 1970), p. 104.

of the sitter, in his late works all the incidentals are dispensed with and the true nature of the individual confronting us is shown. The artistic means employed become even simpler, the color is reduced largely to black and white, yet no artist has ever used them so effectively and with greater subtlety and strength. The brushstrokes become more pronounced and more visible, especially in the light passages.

The earliest picture in this style is the male portrait in The Metropolitan Museum of Art, which Slive dates 1650 to 1652. However, many other paintings from this phase of Hals's career can be found in leading European and American museums, works such as the magnificent portrait of Tyman Oosdorp in the Dahlem Museum in Berlin, painted in 1656 when the artist was seventy-one, and the likeness of William Croes in the Alte Pinakothek in Munich. But the culminating efforts of the artist's old age are the two group portraits done in 1664 of the *Governors of the Old Men's Alms House*, which are now in the Frans Hals Museum in Haarlem. Painted when the artist was almost eighty, these pictures show the master at his best and most profound. Although the theme of six

*Frans Hals*
Male Portrait
*1650–1652*
*Courtesy The Metropolitan*
*Museum of Art,*
*Gift of Henry Marquand, 1890,*
*New York*

*This* Male Portrait *of 1650–1652*
*by Frans Hals was completed in*
*the sixty-seventh year of the*
*artist's life.*

men and five women seated at a table is a traditional one and had been treated by many Dutch artists of the time, Hals brings to this subject a freshness and brilliance that are not found in the work of any of his contemporaries or even in his own earlier work. Focusing the light on their faces, collars, cuff links, and hands, with much of the rest of the canvas bathed in darkness, he gives them a kind of magic, which Pierre Descargues has described in these words: "He carried them with him into a realm where the human being really has no place, and the poor burghers, surprised and surprising, found themselves involved in a profound meditation on death."[23]

In all of the history of painting there are few more creative figures than the great Spanish artist Francisco Goya. Born in 1746 at Fuendetodos near Saragossa and dying in Bordeaux in 1828 at the age of eighty-two, Goya's life spanned the period that saw the end of feudalism and the beginning of the modern age. This is clearly reflected in his work, for his early paintings are in the Rococo style, followed by realistic pictures based on Velazquez, Rembrandt, and themes from nature. His late work reflects the influence of the Romantic movement and anticipates later artistic schools such as Impressionism, Expressionism, and even Surrealism. Having started his artistic career in 1760 at the age of fourteen as an apprentice in the studio of José Luzán, Goya's creative period lasted over six decades, a large part of it spent as a court painter of the Spanish kings in Madrid. While these years were tremendously rich ones and the artist's output was remarkable both in terms of sheer quantity and in the quality of his best production, it was nevertheless in his very last years that some of his greatest paintings and finest prints as well as almost all of his surviving drawings were made.

This late phase of Goya's artistic development is usually said to have begun in the year 1819, when the seventy-three-year-old artist fell gravely ill and bought a country villa on the outskirts of Madrid. It became known as the Quinta del Sordo or Deaf Man's House. It was on the walls of this house that he painted the most powerful creations of his old age between the years 1820 and 1822, the so-

[23] Pierre Descargues, *Hals* (Geneva: Skira, 1968), p. 122.

called *pinturas negras*, or black pictures, which are justly regarded as among his greatest masterpieces. Painted almost entirely in blacks, grays, and whites in a very sketchy, abstract style, they have a tremendous power and mirror in a very expressive manner the tragic vision of life held by the aged painter. There are altogether fourteen pictures, which originally decorated the walls of the living room on the ground floor and the study upstairs. Later, however, they were detached from the walls and removed to the Prado, where they are now on display. Fantastic, nightmarish scenes with grotesque images, the paintings can best be described as Expressionistic, for they foreshadow the kind of simplification and distortion used by twentieth-century artists to heighten the emotional intensity of their work. The subjects depicted are taken partially from ordinary life but more commonly from Greek mythology, the Bible, and the world of dreams and nightmares. Yet all of them are imbued with the same haunting imagery and are rendered in the same simple, powerful style. The two most impressive are *The Witches' Sabbath*, in which a black goat is seen presiding over a meeting of weird-looking witches painted in bold, loosely applied brushstrokes, and

*Francisco Goya*
Saturn Devouring His Son
*1820–1822*
*Courtesy Museo Del Prado,*
*Madrid*

Saturn Devouring His Son *was*
*painted during Goya's introspective*
*final years.*

above all, the *Saturn Devouring His Son,* perhaps the most chilling of all of Goya's works. In it he depicts the ancient Greek myth of the god Saturn, who had been told that one of his children would kill and replace him, devouring his son, whom he holds in his powerful hands. The youth's head has already been bitten off and Saturn is shown removing one of the arms and eating it. The mad eyes and frenzied expression of the face and body of the god, rendered in broad strokes almost entirely in black and white with just a few highlights in color, are truly terrifying and show Goya at the very height of his power.

Such was the creative energy and vitality of the artist that only two years later in 1824, when he was seventy-eight years old, he painted pictures in a completely new and very different style, resembling that employed by the Impressionists fifty years later. He had in the meantime fled Spain to escape the repressive regime of Ferdinand VII and moved to Bordeaux, where he spent most of the remainder of his life. In spite of being almost eighty, completely deaf, and in poor health, he continued to study and experiment, taking up the new artistic medium of lithography and painting some of his loveliest pictures. Two late drawings of Goya's, one showing an old man writing intently in a book in which is written "you knew a lot but you are still learning," and the other representing very old bearded men hobbling on sticks saying, "I am still learning," may well represent Goya himself in his extreme old age, living in exile and close to death, but still growing and learning and producing some of the most original works of his entire career.[24]

The finest of these very late canvases painted in France and now in the Prado is the *Milkmaid of Bordeaux*, which, as Pierre Gassier in his study of Goya says, is ". . . one of his tenderest works, representing a pretty girl with parted lips and dreamy eyes, languorous and pensive. After so many fierce and somber works born of tragic experience, Goya revels for the last time in the whole scale of greens and blues, luminous and translucent."[25] Other outstanding paintings of his final years are the magnificent portraits such as that of Don José Pío de Molina, which was painted in his very last year and is now in the Reinhart Collection in Winterthur, and that of Santiago Galos in the Barnes Collection in Philadelphia. Even more striking, and clearly reflecting the creativity and curiosity of the aged artist, are a series of still lifes that he is believed to have painted at the vegetable market in Bordeaux. In their informality and freshness, they seem more the work of a young Impressionist painter than that of a very old man who was born during the middle of the eighteenth century and was close to his death.

Equally impressive are the prints of Goya's old age. In fact, some of the finest of all of the graphic works of the artist date from the last decade of his life. The most powerful of these are a series of twenty-two etchings entitled *Disparates*, or *Proverbs*, which were

[24] E. A. Sayre, "An Old Man Writing," Bulletin of the Boston Museum of Fine Arts, vol. LVI, 1958, p. 117.
[25] Pierre Gassier, *Goya*, translated by J. Emmons (New York: Skira, 1955), p. 123.

made between the years 1820 and 1824, that is, between his seventy-fourth and seventy-eighth years. The same dark, nightmare vision seen in his black paintings is reflected. Executed with great skill and showing a strange and haunting imagination, they are among the greatest masterpieces in the entire history of graphic arts. In them a world of fantasy inhabited by ghosts and monsters, and the influences of horror, sadism, and superstition find powerful and sinister expression. As Goya saw it, the world was a mad and brutal place in which people, as he shows them in one print, are sitting on a rotten branch, listening to an orator, unaware that the branch could break at any minute and they might all perish. Another print shows a doctor feeling the pulse of a patient who is a donkey, with the inscription "Of What Will He Die?", indicating what fools we humans are. In yet other etchings, men are shown carried off by winged monsters or attempting to fly, cruel people deride blind men, and a woman is being attacked by a wild horse that she is riding. Rendered in a simple but immensely powerful style, these images springing deeply out of Goya's unconscious are among his most vivid creations. Many attempts have been made to explain them, but they have ultimately defied all rational analysis.

In a way, the most amazing of Goya's graphic works are his series of bullfight prints, the *Toros de Burdeos*, of 1825. Executed in a completely new print technique, lithography, when he was eighty years old, they show what a remarkably inventive artist Goya was even at this age. Here, as in his late paintings, it would seem that the artist, after coming to France and breathing the freer, fresher air of that country, had experienced a new lease on life. These prints are far superior to the earlier *Tauromachia* series of 1815 and represent his final tribute to the Spanish national institution to which he was very devoted. Treated in a very loose, Impressionistic manner, the scenes are portrayed with great vividness, emphasizing light and movement in contrast to the greater detail and the tonal efforts of the earlier series. Using lithography to its best advantage, Goya produced shortly before his death the first masterpieces in this medium, indicating in this field also the astonishing creativity of this great genius even in his extreme old age.

Two outstanding examples of nineteenth-century artists whose later work has rightly been considered among their most outstanding achievements are Turner and Monet. In both cases, contemporary opinion had reservations about the works of their old age. In fact, many of Turner's canvases that are much admired today were considered incomplete at the time and were not exhibited during his life, while Monet's *Waterlilies* series, which are today considered masterpieces, had remained in his studio and were only rediscovered in recent decades. It would almost seem as if the final artistic statements of these two great painters were too esoteric to be appreciated by their contemporaries, and it took twentieth-century artistic taste and sensibility to see their true value and realize that it was in these pictures of their old age that Turner (1775–1851) and Monet (1840–1926) expressed their most personal and profound vision of nature.

The change in Turner's style occurred during the last two decades of his life, between about 1835, when he was sixty years old, and the time of his death at seventy-six in 1851. It was during these years that he developed the highly individual and abstract style that is characteristic of his old age. As Lawrence Gowing said, "We are aware that in his paintings something singular and incomparable happened. It astounded and bewildered his contemporaries and it is still not altogether comprehensible today. In the pictures that Turner showed—and concealed—in the last two decades of his life a change was evidently taking place of a kind that is disturbing to the artist's public. The critic who wrote in 1839 of imagination and reality striving for mastery in Turner's works was in no doubt that reality was suffering a lamentable defeat. It is evident that both the kind of reality and the order of imagination that painting had traditionally offered were changing in Turner's hands."[26] This development was not an abrupt one but is foreshadowed in his earlier paintings. The turning point can probably be traced to an event that occurred in 1835—the burning of the houses of Parliament in London. The colorful drama that unfolded in front of Turner's eyes inspired the artist to make many on-the-spot sketches of the magnifi-

[26] Lawrence Gowing, *Turner: Imagination and Reality* (New York: Doubleday, 1966), p. 7.

*Joseph Mallord William Turner*
Burning of the Houses of Parliament
*1834–1835*
*Courtesy Cleveland Museum of Art, Bequest of John L. Severance*

*Turner painted* Burning of the Houses of Parliament *in 1835*
*at the age of sixty.*

cent spectacle of the red and yellow flames against the dark blue sky
and led to the creation of some of his finest paintings, such as the
*Burning of the Houses of Parliament* now in the Cleveland Museum
of Art. While based on the actual scene he observed in Westminster
on that October night in 1835, his concern was not so much with the
buildings or the setting, but primarily with the play of color and
light. The tendency that was to become even more pronounced in
the works of his last years is already clearly seen in this picture,
which marks the beginning of his *Altersstil*. Turner's late style,
which some of the more conservative and insensitive of his contemporary critics failed to appreciate or ridiculed outright, became
more fully developed in the following years and resulted in great
masterpieces such as *Peace: Burial at Sea* of 1842, with its magnificent use of blacks and grays, now in the Tate Gallery in London; the
*Snow Storm—Steamboat off a Harbour's Mouth* of the same year;

and his most famous painting, *Rain, Steam and Speed* of 1844, now in the National Gallery in London, to which Turner bequeathed it at the time of his death.

The tendency of the artist to reduce the forms of nature to a symphony of tones in which light and color take on a life of their own is most clearly seen in Turner's watercolors, in which his artistic style finds its purest expression. In his gouaches painted during the 1830s at the estate of his patron Lord Egremont at Petworth and in his sketches of Venice, he was able to express himself even more freely and spontaneously. It is therefore not surprising to be told that he often submitted almost blank canvases to the showings at the Royal Academy and largely painted the pictures on the so-called varnishing days when, as a contemporary observer wrote to a friend, "He finished the *Burning of the Two Houses of Parliament* on the walls the last two days before the Gallery opened to the public. I am told it was good fun to see the great man working away with about fifty surprised stupid apes standing around him, and I understand he was cursedly annoyed—the fools kept peeping into his color box, and examining all his brushes and colors."[27] Other accounts tell of his arriving at the Royal Academy in the morning, working frantically all day with a few small brushes and a small box of colors, and walking away when he had finished, without even a backward glance. The sight of the aged Turner thus completing his canvases in public view became a famous sight, which many people watched in awe and amazement.

However, even more puzzling to his contemporaries were his very last pictures that even his greatest admirer and early advocate John Ruskin, who had done so much to establish his reputation, failed to appreciate. Even today scholars are not quite certain if the canvases he did during his final years are finished or were looked upon as incomplete by the artist. As Gowing says, "The evidence of what he considered finished is conflicting. He showed regularly in his last decades pictures that contemporaries thought unfinished and at least one of the early pictures that he reworked for exhibition was reduced to a state as amorphous as anything here."[28] Most of these

[27] Ibid., p. 42.
[28] Ibid., p. 36.

pictures, now in the Tate Gallery with the rest of the Turner bequest, are believed to have been painted during the 1840s when the artist was in his late sixties and seventies. The chief theme he treated in these was the sea, which seems to have exerted an endless fascination for him. *Sun Setting Over the Sea, Sunrise with Seamonster* or *Seascape* are characteristic titles given to these paintings, in which, embodying his ultimate vision of nature, the sea is dissolved into pure atmosphere, light, and above all, color.

Monet's old-age style can be dated as beginning in 1898, when the artist began to paint his pictures depicting the garden at Giverny near Paris, and ending with his death in 1926. As he was born in 1840, he was almost sixty at the time. The first exhibition of these works was held in 1900 when he showed a group of canvases depicting his water garden and the Japanese footbridge. It was from the bridge that he contemplated the waterlilies, which in subsequent years became his chief and all-consuming subject matter. What the sea had been for Turner, these flowers became for Monet in his old age. While he did paint other subjects, notably Venetian scenes and views of London, it was to the depiction of the waterlilies that he turned again and again.

Like the old Rembrandt, Monet at this stage of his life, a lonely and unhappy man after the death of his wife in 1911 and that of his son in 1914, had all but ceased painting and in 1917 had developed a cataract in one eye. He complained to the dealer René Gimpel, "I am half blind and deaf." He continued working in spite of this, but in 1922 he was suffering from double cataracts and was losing his sight entirely, but, as he said, he was trying to "paint everything before he could no longer see anything at all."[29] However, an operation restored his vision at least partially in one eye, and he resumed painting with undiminished vigor in spite of experiencing depression and discouragement. In a letter to his friend Gustave Geffroy he wrote, "I have painted for half a century and will soon have passed my sixty-ninth year, but, far from decreasing, my sensibility has sharpened with age . . . I have nothing to fear from old

[29] R. Goldwater and M. Treves, *Artists on Art* (New York: Pantheon, 1945), p. 313.

age. I have no other wish than a close fusion with nature and I desire no other fate than (according to Goethe's precept) to have worked and lived in harmony with the laws."[30]

Like Turner, Monet in these works of his old age turned away from depicting nature as we see it in ordinary life. The Realism of his early period, and even the Impressionism of his maturity, gave way to a more abstract vision of reality in which the objects depicted are less and less important and the colors and shapes assume a life of their own. The pictures that bring about the culmination of his old-age style are the group of large canvases of waterlilies for which he built a large new studio in 1916 at the age of seventy-six. Working frantically with wholehearted dedication, he produced a series of mural-size canvases, which were placed in a circle around the walls of the glass-roofed interior, forming a panorama of waterlilies, water, light, and sky. Talking to René Gimpel and Georges Bernheim, who visited Monet in his studio at this time, he said, "All day long I work on these canvases, I am brought one after the other. In the atmosphere, a color reappeared that I have found yesterday, and sketched on one of the canvases. Quickly the picture is passed to me and I endeavor so far as possible to fix the vision definitely; but usually it disappears so rapidly that it has passed to make way for another color introduced several days ago in another study that is placed before me almost instantly—and it continues like that all day."[31]

From then on, practically all of Monet's work dealt with the waterlily theme and with the rendering of the Japanese footbridge, to which he devoted a strangely intense and very abstract series of pictures painted between 1919 and 1922, at the time he was having the most trouble with his eyes. These canvases, which seemed completely incomprehensible then, seem to have foreshadowed Abstract Expressionism and have only been appreciated in recent years. However, more typical of the output of Monet's extreme old age, for he was a man in his eighties at the time, is the famous set of twelve waterlily canvases he gave to the French state, which are now in the

[30] William C. Seitz, ed., *Claude Monet, Seasons and Moments* (New York: Abrams, 1960), p. 58.
[31] Ibid., p. 154.

*Claude Monet*
Water Lilies
*c. 1920*
*Courtesy Collection, Museum of Modern Art,*
*Mrs. Simon Guggenheim Fund, New York*

*Monet painted his beautiful Abstract-Impressionist* Water Lilies
*in 1920 at eighty, as he approached the end of his life.*

Orangerie in Paris, and the magnificent triptych that he painted
around 1920, now in the collection of The Museum of Modern Art
in New York. The style of these works is perhaps best described as
Abstract Impressionist, and it is not pure chance that these paintings, after years of neglect, were only rediscovered during the
1950s, when they were shown to enthusiastic audiences in Paris,
Zurich, the Hague, London, and New York.

Although already a man of eighty, Monet continued painting
to the day of his death at the age of eighty-six in 1926. Having
outlived all his contemporaries and not much appreciated by the
young artists of the day, who had embraced new artistic styles such
as Fauvism, Cubism, and Expressionism, the master continued pour-
ing out magnificent canvases that today are regarded as among the
supreme masterpieces of his entire career. He was haunted by the
desire to express what he was "trying to realize" and as he put it, he
did not wish to die before he had said "everything that I have to
say—or at least having tried to say it."[32] Defying old age, infirmity,
and discouragement, which at one point led him to burn six canvases
with which he was dissatisfied, Monet, looking like an Old Testament prophet with a long, white beard, continued creating images
that reflected his inner vision rather than merely recording nature,

[32] B. Delange, "Claude Monet", *L'Illustration*, vol. 169 June 1927, p. 54.

which at this stage of his life he could see only incompletely. And while some no doubt prefer his youthful paintings executed in a clearer and more precise style, and others see him primarily as the most consistent and typical painter of the Impressionist movement, there are those among contemporary critics and artists who see his final works as the most profound and beautiful manifestation of his genius.

The third of the great nineteenth-century painters who had a true old-age style was Cézanne. Like Rembrandt, at least by our modern standards, he never became very old, for he died at the age of sixty-seven. However, the ten years, from 1895 until his death in 1906, represent a distinct period in regard to both his life and his art. Suffering from diabetes, which accentuated his irritability and emotional outbursts, "nearly decrepit by the age of sixty, Cézanne was prematurely old."[33] In 1899 the artist talked of old age having caught up with him, and in a letter of 1903 he said he was very tired. In 1905, when he was only sixty-six, he referred to himself as almost seventy.[34] And yet these afflictions of his old age in no way interfered with his creative efforts. His devotion to his work remained undiminished to the day of his death. In fact, his death came as a result of catching pneumonia after being drenched by rain while on a painting expedition. In his studio he had written as his motto "Happiness is work," and it was in that spirit that he spent his days, dedicated increasingly to the ardent and often frustrating pursuit of an artistic vision that he felt was almost in his grip. If there is truth in Goethe's dictum at the end of *Faust*, that he who strives unceasingly will be saved, there can be no doubt that Cézanne will be one of the elect.

At this late stage of his artistic career a measure of success was finally coming Cézanne's way and Vollard was showing his work, beginning with an exhibition at his gallery in 1895, which aroused considerable attention on the part of the younger artists and even

[33] Jack Lindsay, *Cézanne, His Life and Art* (Greenwich, Conn.: New York Graphic Society), p. 287.
[34] *Paul Cézanne's Letters*, ed. by John Rewald (New York: Hacker, 1976), pp. 268 and 294.

led to purchases by some of the more discriminating and adventurous collectors. Astonishingly, Cézanne's self-image still remained uncertain, fluctuating from absolute certainty that he was the greatest painter of the age or, as he once said in a moment of exuberance, "the only one," to darker moods in which he referred to himself as a terrible failure who had been totally unsuccessful as an artist. Writing to his friend Claude Monet in 1895, he talks of having returned to the south, "From which I should, perhaps, never have been separated in order to fling myself into the chimerical pursuit of art."[35] However, at other times he saw clearly that he was a great pioneer, who, since he was ahead of his time, had perhaps arrived too early. As he wrote to a young artist, "I was a painter of your generation more than my own."[36]

Nevertheless, it was during these last years of his life, especially the opening years of the twentieth century, that Cézanne, much ridiculed and totally neglected by his fellow citizens of the provincial southern French town of Aix in which his father was a highly regarded, successful banker with no appreciation of his son's genius, finally gained recognition. He wrote to the critic Roger Marx, who was an ardent admirer of his, "My age and health will never allow me to realize my dream of art that I have been pursuing all my life. But I shall always be grateful to the public of intelligent amateurs who in spite of my hesitations have intuitively understood what I wanted to try in order to renew art. To my mind one does not put oneself in place of the past, one only adds a new link, with a painter's temperament and an artistic ideal, that is to say, a conception of nature; sufficient powers of expression would have been necessary to be intelligible to the general public and to occupy a fitting position in the history of art."[37]

Surrounded at the end of his life by ardent young followers who hailed him as a master in whose footsteps they would follow, Cézanne finally realized that his life had not been lived in vain, although the "bourgeois from Aix" part of him continued to resent that the Salons were not welcoming him, that the critics by and large

[35] Ibid, p. 242.
[36] Ibid., p. 255.
[37] Ibid., p. 313.

remained hostile, and that the Legion of Honor had not been given to him.

Encouraged by the late recognition and feeling that he was finally being understood and appreciated by at least some artists and critics, Cézanne produced during the last years of his life some of his finest paintings, which in a way bring about the culmination of his life's work. Roger Fry was the first really to appreciate this phase of his artistic career when he wrote, "It would appear that there was at the end of Cézanne's life a recrudescence of the impetuous, romantic exuberance of his early youth. There is nothing wanton or willful about it, nothing of the defiant gesture of that period, but there is a new impetuosity in the rhythms, a new exaltation in the color. This is of course a well-known phenomenon among artists who live to an advanced age. Titian's is the classic example."[38] Returning, as Fry says, to the more romantic and emotional vein of his early period and to a certain extent moving away from the more classical mood of his mature work, Cézanne in these late works combined the intensity of the former with the formal grandeur of the latter, thereby establishing a new kind of emotional quality and aesthetic unity representing a complete new phase of his life's work. The main means of artistic expression becomes his colors, with blues and greens predominating, and through color alone the aged artist is able to give his paintings a beauty and strength that is unique in the painting of his time. In these canvases of his last years, especially in the great landscapes, Cézanne, basing himself on nature and always trying to achieve a fuller realization of the natural vision, sums up the artistic achievement of the nineteenth century. At the same time, in his ability to simplify and abstract, he anticipates much of the art of the twentieth.

It is very difficult to date these pictures, as he often worked upon several canvases simultaneously and his late work has neither a stylistic unity nor a progressive development.[39] However, it is evident that his concerns change dramatically and even though he continues to paint the same artistic motifs, notably Mont Ste. Vic-

---

[38] Roger Fry, *Cezanne, A Study of His Development* (New York: Macmillan, 1952), p. 80.
[39] K. Badt: *Das Spätwerk Cezannes* (Konstanz: Konstanzer Universitätsreden, 1971).

Le Chateau Noir, *one of Cézanne's great final landscapes, was completed*
*two years before his death in 1906 at the age of sixty-seven.*

toire as well as still lifes, portraits, and figure compositions, they
take on a character very different from that of his earlier work. The
landscapes above all express this new spirit best. Having in these last
years built a studio for himself at Les Lauves, north of Aix, from
which he had a magnificent view of the mountains, he painted his
beloved motif of the majestic mountains surrounding Aix over and
over again. Meyer Schapiro, writing about one of these pictures
(*Mont Ste. Victoire* in the Tyson Collection) painted between 1904
and 1906, uses the following words:

> It is a stormy rhapsody in which earth, mountain and sky are
> united in a common paean, an upsurge of color, of rich tones

on a vast scale. It is an irrepressible lyric fulfillment which reminds one of Beethoven's music. The dynamism of fervid emotion possesses the entire canvas. The contrasts are not simply stable and unstable, as in other works, but different kinds of movement and intense color. The mountain rises passionately to the sky and also glides on the earth. Its surface is like a perspective network of ascending lines, converging to a peak as a goal. The sky in turn bursts into a dance of colors, an explosion of clouds of blue and green, tremendous volumes of sonorous color which form a tempestuous halo of pure tones around the glorious mountain and give the latter a more living, dramatic quality. The earth approaches chaos, yet is formed of clear verticals and horizontal strokes in sharp contrast to the diagonal strokes of the mountain and the many curving strokes of the sky. These reappear in the lower foreground in blues and purples and violets, a reversed echo of the distant mountain. Under all this turbulence of the brushwork and color lies the grand horizontal expanse of the earth.[40]

A similar intensification of emotion and mastery of color for expressive purpose may also be found in the late still lifes and portraits, which now have a depth of feeling not found in his earlier work. Beginning with the picture of his friend Gustave Geffroy in 1895 and especially in the portraits of simple people of Aix, such as his gardener Villier, Cézanne brings to these depictions of fellow human beings a kind of emotional quality absent from those of his classical period. And throughout these last years he continued working on what he felt was the most important and ambitious undertaking of his life, the completion of the grand *Bathers*, which took up the great tradition where his beloved Venetians and Poussin had left off. It was a formidable task on which he spent ten years and in which he felt he was not wholly successful. While some of the smaller versions of this theme succeed magnificently, the ultimate masterpiece worthy of the Baroque tradition escaped him. However, during these same years, in a very different medium and on a much smaller scale, he created unique and wholly perfect pictures,

[40] Meyer Schapiro, ed., *Paul Cézanne* (New York: Abrams, 1952), p. 22.

namely, in the field of watercolors. All that he was striving for was realized in a very simple and natural way in these paintings. With a few brushstrokes, leaving much of the paper blank and using the greatest economy of means, as the great Chinese masters of this art form had done, he created some of the most beautiful of all his works. They can stand beside the greatest watercolor paintings of any period or civilization.

Of the twentieth-century artists, it is Henri Matisse above all who developed a distinct old-age style and produced some of the most beautiful works of his entire career during his seventies and eighties. Unlike Cézanne, he reached a ripe old age, dying in 1954 when he was eighty-five. Born in 1869, he had a long and very eventful life, experiencing as a young man the beginning of the modern movement in which he was to be a leader and living through both the First and Second World War. Although he had a serious operation in 1941 and was bedridden during the last years of his life, he continued creating artistic masterpieces reflecting his joy in life and love of beauty. While there were artists who in their final years fathomed spiritual depths far more profound than those Matisse expressed, he was unique in giving vent to the same joyousness and exuberance when he was a crippled old man as he had done as a young man during his Fauve period.

The late work of Matisse is usually dated from 1939 when he was seventy years old. Too old to take an active part in the war, he fled to southern France, where he settled near Nice, first in Vence and later in Cimiez, where he is buried. In spite of the hardships of those years both for France and for his own family, Matisse's canvases of the 1940s were hymns to joy—interiors, figure pieces, and still lifes painted in bright colors with a fine sense of decorative design and pattern. The culmination of this series is found in *The Large Interior in Red* of 1948 in the Musée de l'Art Moderne in Paris. The exhibition of these works in this museum in 1949, to mark the artist's eightieth birthday, created a sensation. It was one of the most oustanding artistic events of the immediate postwar period and won the aged artist many new admirers.

As Matisse's health deteriorated and he was unable to stand at the easel, he was forced to employ other forms of artistic expression, notably paper cutouts, a medium in which he did much of the finest work of his last years. He had already used large movable cutouts in planning the murals for the Barnes Foundation in 1931, but it was really not until the late 1940s and above all the 1950s that he used this type of work extensively. Matisse saw these cutouts as a mere continuation of his painting. He said, "There is no break between my painting and my cutouts. Only with something more of the ab-

*Henri Matisse*
Beasts of the Sea
*1950*
*Courtesy National Gallery of Art,*
*Alisa Mellon Bruce Fund,*
*Washington, D.C.*

Beasts of the Sea, *done in 1950 when Matisse was eighty-one, is just one of the many fine cutouts the infirm artist created during the last years of his life.*

stract and the absolute, I have arrived at a distillation of form. . . .
Cutting paper permits me to draw in color, for one it is a matter of
simplification. Instead of establishing contour, and then filling it
with colors—the one modifying the other—I draw directly in color.
. . . This generates a precise union of the two processes. They become one."[41]

In spite of his physical handicaps and the limitations of the
medium, Matisse achieved in these works some of his finest creations. He used large scissors to cut colored pieces of paper, which
were then mounted on the wall by assistants. The result was designs
of a simplicity and grandeur that even he had only rarely equaled
before. Using the forms of nature but simplifying them, he reduced
them to their very essence in a timeless, ultimate way. The largest of
these cutouts, the fifty-foot-long *Swimming Pool* of 1952, now in
The Museum of Modern Art in New York, is among his most ambitious compositions, yet even the smaller ones representing nudes,
flowers, and semiabstract forms are impressive. In 1958, *Verve*
magazine, for which he designed covers, devoted a special issue to
these works of his last years that had served as a source of inspiration and aesthetic pleasure to a whole generation of younger artists.

In addition to the cutouts, Matisse also devoted himself in these
last years to a project he regarded as the culminating artistic enterprise of his old age, the decoration of the Chapel of the Rosary at
Vence. From 1948 to 1951 he concentrated almost wholly on this
work, planning both the exterior and interior architecture and above
all the decoration of the walls, windows, and altar of the sanctuary,
even designing the vestments worn by the priest. The inspiration for
this religious undertaking came from two Dominican nuns, Sister
Marie-Ange, who had nursed him after his operation in 1941, and
Sister Marie Jacques, who had taken care of him in his later years.
Although he was not a practicing Catholic or even religious in a
traditional sense, he wished to create a spiritual atmosphere in keeping with the faith to which the chapel was dedicated. Using a simple,
very plain linear style, he painted the figures of the Virgin and
Child, St. Dominique, and the Via Crucis on the walls, produced

[41] M. Wheeler, *The Last Works of Henri Matisse* (New York: The Museum of
Modern Art, 1961), p. 10.

colored designs for the stained-glass windows, and made a sculpture of the crucified Christ for the altar. The result was a work of great simplicity and purity of expression that is considered one of the religious masterpieces of the twentieth century.

No discussion of the work of Matisse's old age would be complete without saying something about his prints and drawings. Among these are the beautiful series of color cutouts called *Jazz*, made in 1947 when he was already seventy-eight. They were reproduced in color lithography. And the numerous ink sketches executed in a bold, heavy line show the vigor and remarkable draftsmanship he still possessed in his last years. As Giuseppe Marchiori said, "Matisse never suffered the decline of old age and its progressive sterilization of the creative facilities. He was driven by an energy, courage and faith in life which enabled him to find new means of expression in constant experimentation aimed at achieving the essential."[42]

[42] Giuseppe Marchiori, *Matisse: The Artist and His Time* (New York: Reynal, 1967), p. 103.

# 2 THE LAST IS THE BEST

$A$ second significant group of creative artists is comprised of those who did their best work during the last decades of their lives. This is a phenomenon that can be observed particularly during the modern era but is not unknown in earlier periods and civilizations. It may be that these artists were slow to mature and only developed their full potential late in life or that the circumstances under which they lived proved more conducive to artistic creativity during their later years. However, there can be no doubt that artists of this type have existed in the past and are encountered today, although it should be added at once that the opposite is far more frequent—artists who show great promise in their youth but lose their inspiration as they grow older.

The turning point in most of these cases, as was also true of those who had a distinctive old-age style, seems to have been at about age sixty, when in the lives of many people a new stage in their development seems to take place. Whether this is a culturally conditioned phenomenon or has some biological or physiological basis is difficult to determine. However, since several of the most notable artists who reached the apex of their artistic creativity in old age are to be found among Chinese, Japanese, and Islamic artists, it would appear that it certainly is not a wholly modern Western phenomenon resulting from the peculiar social and cultural conditions prevailing in Europe and America at the present time.

The most notable example of such an artist is no doubt the Japanese painter and printmaker Katsushika Hokusai (1760–1849), who lived a long and immensely productive life during which he is said to have produced more than thirty thousand designs. Yet as Hokusai himself said in looking back over his artistic career, "I have been in love with painting ever since I became conscious of it at the age of six. I drew some pictures I thought fairly good when I was fifty, but really nothing I did before the age of seventy was of any value at all. At seventy-three I have at last caught every aspect of nature—birds, fish, animals, insects, trees, grasses, all. When I am eighty I shall have developed still further, and I will really master the secrets of art at ninety. When I reach a hundred my work will be truly sublime, and my final goal will be attained around the age of one hundred and ten, when every line and dot I draw will be imbued with life."[1]

Unfortunately we cannot judge what Hokusai's work was like at one hundred or at one hundred ten, the time when he hoped to reach perfection, since he died in 1849 at what, by Japanese reckoning, would have been ninety. However, there can be no doubt that, as he said, it was only at fifty that he reached his artistic maturity and that almost all of the work on which his reputation rests today was made after his sixtieth year. In 1833, when he was a man of seventy-three, he called himself Gakyo-rojin, "Art-Crazy Old Man," indicating that it was at this stage of his life that he felt most truly absorbed in his art. And when he was on his deathbed, he lamented that if he had only been granted ten or even five years longer to live, he might have become a great artist.

Although Hokusai had produced a vast number of prints, paintings, sketches, and illustrated books before his sixtieth birthday, it

[1] I. Kondo, *Katsushika Hokusai,* English text by E. Grilli (Tokyo: Charles E. Tuttle Co., 1955), p. 13.

was only during his last three decades that the masterpieces that represent the culmination of his life's work were created. Beginning in 1823, when he started his most famous series of colored wood-block prints, *The Thirty-six Views of Mt. Fuji*, and continuing to the end of his life, he produced splendid works, many of them when he was in his seventies and eighties. Events such as his exile between 1834 and 1836, the famine which hit Edo (present-day Tokyo) in 1836, and the great fire of 1839, which destroyed his house and many of his pictures, failed to curb his artistic creativity. In fact, they only spurred the aged artist on to ever greater activity.

Works such as the *Red Fuji, Fuji in Lightning*, and *Fuji Beneath the Great Wave* are universally regarded as among his finest prints and as masterpieces in this art form, yet they were made when Hokusai was already an old man and represent not the end but the beginning of the most creative phase of his artistic development. This celebrated set, which originally contained thirty-six prints, to which ten more were added when it proved so popular, was completed in 1829, when the artist was seventy, and it was followed almost at once by a new series depicting the sacred mountain, called *Hundred Views of Mt. Fuji*, which was published in 1834. It consisted of three volumes of black-and-white prints of excellent quality, which, although not as famous as the earlier set, show the same wonderful sense of design and fine feeling for nature that had marked the earlier Fuji prints.

Other celebrated prints produced by the master during these years were devoted to the picturesque waterfalls of Japan, famous bridges, views of the Lu Chu Islands, images of the poets of China and Japan, and especially pictures of birds and flowers, which some critics consider his best work.

During the last years of his life, when he was past seventy, he continued to pour out an endless stream of paintings, sketches, illustrated books, greeting cards, or *surimono*, and prints. Among those, the numerous depictions of ghosts and goblins, the series entitled *The Hundred Tales*, and the *Hundred Views of Mt. Fuji* were the most outstanding. His last great series, called *Hundred Poems Explained by the Nurse*, which was started in 1839, when he was eighty, shows him still in full command of his powers. And when he was close to ninety, he collaborated with young contemporaries in

*Katsushika Hokusai*
The Kirifuri Waterfall
*Series:* Travels to the Waterfalls
  of the Various Provinces
*c. 1827–1830*
*Courtesy Nelson-Atkins Museum*
*of Art,*
*Nelson Fund,*
*Kansas City, Missouri*

*Hokusai described himself as an*
*"art-crazy old man." This print*
*of the Kirifuri Waterfall is from*
*his series* Travels to the
Waterfalls of the Various
Provinces, *thought to have been*
*completed by the artist in his*
*seventieth year.*

producing several books of poetry that were published in 1848 and 1849, the year of his death.

Jack Hillier describes the old artist as he is depicted in the Katsushika Hokusaiden, the testimony of friends and acquaintances of his last years, as follows:

> It is the picture of an old man pathetically alone with art, who had dedicated all his days to drawing and found no time for the graces of living, remaining to the end unsociable and difficult to approach, who neither drank wine nor smoked tobacco, and who only ate enough to keep his hardy old body alive. His only driving force was the urge to draw, not, certainly,

to earn an easy way of life, nor even to win renown, though he was not adverse to recognition; but from an innate propensity to translate everything within his experience, the daily round of men and women, the Yedo scene, the Japanese countryside, story, legend, history and poetry into the language of the brush, a language which we now read and enjoy and think we understand, though separated from him by an abyss of years and a way of life he could not have dreamed of.[2]

The other great figure in the history of Japanese art who did his best work in his old age was Tomioka Tessai, who lived from 1837 to 1924. He is generally regarded as the last of the truly traditional Japanese painters who worked in the Chinese style of ink painting of the so-called Southern school. A man deeply steeped in Confucianist learning, he was one of the literati painters of the school known in Japan as Bunjin-ga. At the same time he also served for a time as a Shinto priest, a period that he referred to as the happiest of his life. Although he took up painting as early as 1861, in his twenty-fourth year, it was really not until 1896, when he was sixty, that he enjoyed enough patronage to depend exclusively on painting for his livelihood. As his biographer Taro Odakane says, "It was not until 1907 that he was at the height of his creative greatness; incisive in the boldness of his vision, his vital native talents propelled by the momentum of decades of diligent concentration and practice. He was the master of all the traditional brush handling techniques, and he had finally acquired a stature among proponents of the Bunjin-ga style as one of the outstanding members of the tradition."[3]

Working during the Meiji and Taisho periods, a time when Japanese painting was increasingly influenced by Western art, Tessai remained true to the older Far Eastern tradition of ink painting, so that when the German scholar Curt Glaser visited him in 1911, he proclaimed Tessai's work the very essence of the Oriental pictorial tradition. And far from diminishing in creative power during his extreme old age, it is generally conceded that it was during his eigh-

---

[2] Jack Hillier, *Hokusai* (London: Phaidon Press, 1955), p. 125.

[3] Taro Odakane, *Tomioka Tessai* (Tokyo and Rutland, Vt.: Charles E. Tuttle, 1956), p. 24.

*Tomioka Tessai*
Mountain Landscape
*Meiji Period, c. 1907*
*Courtesy Collection of National Museum,*
*Tokyo*

*This picture was painted when the artist was*
*about seventy-five years old.*

ties that he did his best work. James Cahill had this to say about it in
his catalog of the 1972 Nanga show at the Asia House Gallery in
New York: "Tessai's most brilliant productions are those of his very
last years; he painted prolifically until his death at the age of eighty-
nine. In these late works he uses inks lavishly, in a way analogous to
recent Western expressionist painters' impasto use of oils, for powerful compositions that typically build vertically within the picture
space with no real attempt to establish any depth beyond occasional
hollows and narrow openings."[4] And it was especially between
1920 and 1924, when the artist was nearing his ninetieth birthday,

[4] James Cahill, *Scholar Painters of Japan, The Nanga School* (New York: Asia
House Gallery, 1972), p. 124.

that he did his most expressive and beautiful pictures. He continued working to the last day of his life with undiminished vigor, producing masterpieces of traditional ink painting that surpassed his earlier work as well as anything being done by his younger colleagues. As his friend and most passionate patron and advocate Bishop Sakamoto, the abbot of the Kiyoshi Kojin Seicho temple, recalls, "He approached the spring of his ninetieth year with increasing vigor; then on the last day of the last month of the year, he departed for another world, ending gladly his long and peaceful mortal life. Until the end, his brushwork did not decline, but rather manifested an energy which seemed to transcend human bounds." He adds, "His death was all the more to be regretted."[5] It is on the paintings of these last years, when he was a man in his eighties, that his great reputation rests today, and his fame and popularity have increased considerably both in his native country and abroad since his death some fifty years ago.

Another outstanding artist in the non-Western tradition who did his most significant work long after the age when most people are thinking of retirement was the Turkish architect Sinan, or Ibn Abd al Mannan. The greatest single figure in the history of Islamic architecture, Sinan was born in 1489 and is said to have lived to extreme old age, dying either in 1578 at eighty-nine or more likely in 1588 at the age of ninety-nine. The later date, which is accepted by most scholars, is based on the testimony of Mustafa Sai. Sinan had an immensely long professional career of some fifty years, and he is said to have designed over three hundred buildings, of which one hundred were mosques. His contribution was very significant, for he produced many of the masterpieces of Ottoman architecture. Although he started his artistic career as a young man, it was really not until he became chief architect to Suleiman the Magnificent in about 1540, when he was fifty-one years old, that he was given the opportunity to develop his genius to its fullest potential.

It was for this great ruler that he built the Suleimaniye between

[5] R. Sakamoto, Tomioka Tessai Catalogue (Washington, D.C.: International Exhibition Foundation, 1957).

1550 and 1556, his sixty-first to sixty-seventh years, a building many architectural historians regard as the finest mosque in Istanbul. Completed in 1557, almost exactly a thousand years after the erection of Hagia Sophia, it is based on that great Byzantine structure but adapts this type of building to the needs of Islam. Its crowning feature is a 175-foot dome that is one of the most splendid in the entire history of architecture and shows Sinan at the height of his creative power.

While the Suleiman mosque is Sinan's best-loved and most celebrated work, Sinan himself, as Arthur Stratton says in his book on the architect, felt otherwise: "He describes the Suleymaniye as the work of a journeyman, which is to say, of a laborer and craftsman, in this instance an architect, new to his trade. With the Shahzades Mosque, completed two years earlier, in 1548, he had finished his ten years as an apprentice."[6] In other words, in his own eyes it was only in his sixtieth year that he felt he had reached his artistic maturity and as he had forty more years of creativity ahead of him during which he produced some of his greatest masterpieces, this estimate is certainly borne out by his later development. Working for Suleiman's son, the Sultan Selim II, he built what is today considered his culminating achievement—the Imperial Friday Mosque at Edirne, which at that time was the capital of the Ottoman Empire. This building, on which he worked from 1568 to 1574, between his seventy-ninth and eighty-fifth years, represents the supreme achievement of Turkish Islamic architecture, combining a beautiful exterior with a superb spatial effect in its interior.

Even this structure did not represent his final creative effort, for in 1577, at the age of eighty-eight, he designed the Azapkapi Cami and in 1850, at ninety-one, the Kaliz Ali Pasa Cami. The last of his works was the Ramazan Efendi Mosque of 1856, and "He asked his old friend the poet Mustafa Sai Chelebi to carve that date in the inscription over the portal."[7] That was the year of Sinan's last will and testament; he was now ninety-seven and ready to die. However, he lived two more years and died in 1588 when he was almost one hundred years old. He had asked to be buried in the garden of

---

[6] Arthur Stratton, *Sinan* (New York: Scribner, 1972), p. 120.
[7] Ibid., p. 247.

his house, behind the Mosque of Suleiman the Magnificent in Istanbul, to whose adornment he contributed so greatly.

Turning to the art of the Western world, the phenomenon of heightened artistic creativity during old age is particularly marked in the twentieth century while it is rare in earlier periods. It may be that the greater emphasis upon individual expression and originality in modern art favors those who in their old age reach depth of insight and expressive power that they had lacked in their earlier years. Or, possibly, it may be that a far larger percentage of artists live into old age; but the fact is that quite a few of the outstanding artists of the last hundred years produced their most interesting work when they were past sixty, and some of them had their most creative period when they were in their seventies and eighties. This is particularly true of some of the leading German and French painters of the early twentieth century who, under the impact of the Modern movement, produced their best work during their later years.

The first of these was Lovis Corinth, who was born in 1858 and died in 1925. A native of East Prussia, he received a thorough academic training at the Art Academy in Königsberg and Munich and, after some years in Paris, set himself up as an independent artist, first in Munich and then in Berlin. His work of these early years followed the prevailing artistic movements, starting with Realism, followed by plein air painting, and finally Impressionism, of which he became one of the leading German practitioners. While his accomplishments in this field were considerable and merit an important place in the history of German painting, he would hardly be thought of today as one of the most original and powerful of modern painters if he had died in his early fifties.

The decisive experience for him seems to have been a near fatal illness that brought him close to death in 1911, when he was fifty-three. It was after his recovery during the following year that he turned his back on Impressionism and took up a more personal and expressive type of painting. Influenced by artists of the Expressionist movement, which had come into prominence during this period, notably Oskar Kokoschka, whom he much admired, Corinth evolved in his later fifties a new artistic style that was much more in keeping with the art of the new century. This development culminated in the work of his last years, which, for power of expression and beauty of color, surpassed anything he had done during the previous decades.

In 1918, when he was sixty years old, he bought some land in Urfeld at the Walchensee in Bavaria, and it was there that he painted his most beautiful canvases. Transforming the scenes he painted through his own deeply felt emotion and using bold, powerful brushstrokes and brilliant colors, the artist, in a frenzy of creativity, produced a series of sixty-one pictures of the mountain lake that in a way foreshadows the work of the Abstract Expressionist painters of the next generation. And it was not only in his landscapes but also in flower pieces and above all in his self-portraits that his real genius manifested itself during these final years of his life when he was a man in his sixties. There is in these pictures an inwardness and spiritual quality that reminds one of Rembrandt's late self-portraits and that makes these works so memorable. He seems to have been aware of this, for he wrote in his journal a few months before his death, "I have found something new; true art is to portray the unreality. This is the highest."[8] Shortly after this, in 1925, he died at the age of sixty-seven.

Even more striking was Christian Rohlfs, who did his finest work when he was already in his eighties. Born in northern Germany in 1849, he too had started as a painter of the Realistic school and had later turned to Impressionism and Pointillism. While an accomplished artist, who had achieved a certain amount of success in Weimar, where he had first been a student and later a teacher at the Art Academy, he hardly differed from the hundreds of other painters who worked in the current idioms of late nineteenth-century painting. Had he died at fifty he would be remembered today, if at all, as a minor artist of the Weimar school. However, during the

[8] C. Berend-Corinth, *Die Gemälde von Lovis Corinth* (Munich: Prestel Verlag, 1958), p. 14.

early years of the twentieth century he came under the influence first of Van Gogh and then the artists of the Brücke and the Fauve painters, and although a full generation older than these young men, he joined their endeavors to establish a new, modern art that would break decisively with the Realistic conventions of nineteenth-century painting.

His first major show reflecting this new orientation was held in Hagen, Westphalia, at the Folkwang Museum, where under the inspired leadership of its director Professor Karl Ernst Osthaus, an important center of modern art had been established. This exhibition was held in 1909 to honor the artist on his sixtieth birthday, and it was followed by a large retrospective in Weimar in 1910. However, since this was a very conservative town, it met with little critical or commercial success. His favorite subject at this time was the Gothic architecture of the old Westphalian town of Soest with its picturesque houses and churches, which he portrayed in oil and water-color paintings and in very strong black-and-white wood-block prints that are among the best productions of his entire career and surpass anything he had done up to this time.

A large exhibition consisting of 127 works, including oils, watercolors, and prints, at the J. B. Neumann Gallery in Berlin in 1918 helped establish his position as one of the leading figures in modern German art, and the great retrospective of his work held at the National Gallery in Berlin in 1919, on the occasion of his seventieth birthday, gave him national recognition as one of the masters of the Expressionist movement. In his seventies and at the full height of his creative powers, Rohlfs now enjoyed a success and happiness that resulted in some of his greatest pictures. Especially fine are his watercolors of the Thuringian city of Erfurt and his flower pieces.

In 1927, when he was almost eighty, he moved to Ascona in Italian Switzerland, and it was there that he spent the rest of his life with a young wife he married in old age. Although these late years saw the rise of Hitler and the outlawing of modern art in Germany —including his own work, which in 1937 was removed from the museums and declared to be degenerate—he continued to paint with undiminished vigor, producing some of his best paintings. In 1938, when he was eighty-eight years old and close to his death, he painted no less than 137 watercolors, the largest number of works he had

*Christian Rohlfs*
Yucca
*c. 1930s*
*Courtesy Busch-Reisinger Museum,*
*Harvard University,*
*Cambridge, Massachusetts*

*The yucca plant is the subject of*
*this gouache, done during the*
*1930s when the artist was in his*
*eighties.*

ever produced during one year. Even more impressive than the volume of his output was that the quality of these late pictures was outstanding. The richness of color and forms and the light and atmosphere of Ascona offered the artist endless inspiration, and he remained active to his last days, dying in his eighty-ninth year.

Among the French artists of the modern age, the one who showed the most remarkable artistic florescence during his old age was Pierre Bonnard. Born in 1867, he had a distinguished artistic career as a young man, becoming, along with his friends Maurice Denis and Edouard Vuillard, one of the founders of the Nabis group in 1891 when he was only twenty-four, and doing some very fine work in both oil painting and color lithography. A gifted painter whose use of light and color suggested a very late offshoot of the Impressionist movement, Bonnard in 1923 received the Carnegie Prize in Pittsburgh and seemed at this time a very sensitive and gifted artist who was essentially a conservative in an age of revolutionary change.

*Pierre Bonnard*
Dining Room on the Garden
*before 1933*
*Courtesy Collection The Solomon R. Guggenheim Museum, New York*

*Bonnard was in his sixties when he painted the subtle*
Dining Room on the Garden.

It was not until the 1930s, when he was in his sixties, that his mature style developed, and it was only during the last years of his life, especially the decade before his death in 1947 at the age of eighty, that he reached the pinnacle of his artistic career. Works such as his *Nude in the Bath* series, painted in the late 1930s and early 1940s, are among the masterpieces of modern painting and reveal an artist who, although profoundly influenced by Impressionism and Post-Impressionism, had developed a very personal abstract style that differs fundamentally from the one he had employed in his earlier years as well as from the Cubist abstractions of his contemporaries. While his work is firmly anchored in visual reality, it dissolves the forms of nature into almost abstract patterns of glowing color and brilliant light that have a radiance and beauty not found in the work of any other modern artist. As John Rewald said in his catalog for the great Bonnard exhibition of 1948 at The Museum of Modern Art in New York a year after the artist's death: "The works of his last years are not inferior to his early ones in freshness and spontaneity, but their horizon is broadened and their color more intense than ever before. Bonnard gradually extended the gamut of his colorations while at the same time he carried his forms closer to abstraction."[9] Painting the sun-drenched landscape of southern France as well as flower pieces and peaches, which were among his favorite motifs, he transformed the forms of nature into symphonies of color that take on a life of their own.

Commenting on these works of his old age, Bonnard said, "I think that when one is young it is the object, the outside world that fires one's enthusiasm, one is carried away by it. In later life it's something within himself, the need to express an emotion, that leads the painter to choose his point of departure, one form rather than another."[10] Working right up to the time of his death with undiminished vigor and with a tremendous sense of joy in the beauty of the world, Bonnard produced his greatest paintings when in his seventies, pictures that were not only hailed by critics as the culmination of the artist's entire career but were also much admired by younger painters who now saw Bonnard, along with Picasso and Matisse, as one of the great masters of twentieth-century painting.

Another outstanding French painter of the twentieth century who developed to his full potential only in his old age was Jacques Villon. Born Gaston Duchamp in 1875, the young artist was a member of the revolutionary generation who, during the early years of the new century, turned to Cubism and abstract painting. His

[9] John Rewald, *Bonnard* (New York: The Museum of Modern Art, 1948), p. 55.
[10] A. Terrasse, *Bonnard*, translated by S. Gilbert (Geneva: Skira Publishers, 1964), p. 73.

work of this period, while innovative and sensitive and revealing considerable talent, does not as yet show the power and beauty of the paintings of his old age. In fact, after serving five years in the French army during the First World War, Villon, as he now called himself, devoted the 1920s largely to prints, earning his living by making reproductions. It was only during the 1930s, when he was approaching sixty, that the artist returned to painting. However, it was not until the 1940s that he won the acclaim of the critics and the public. Now a man of seventy, Villon finally achieved the recognition that had eluded him earlier. In 1950 he received the Carnegie Award, and in 1956, when he was eighty, the Grand Prix at the Venice Biennale. In the same year the French government commissioned him to design a series of frescoes for the Technical School at Cacha and six stained-glass windows for the cathedral at Metz. In 1961 the American Academy of Arts and Letters elected the eighty-six-year-old artist as a member.

Talking about his work, Villon described it as Cubist-Impressionist. It was indeed in this fusion of what he had learned from Cubism, which he had embraced as a young man in Paris, and a more realistic type of painting that he took up when he left the metropolis and, as he put it, "touched the earth again" in rural France after 1935, that his great achievement lies. A lyrical painter and a subtle colorist, he was able to combine a feeling for geometry and color with a sense of visual reality, resulting in works of great beauty and elegance. Werner Haftmann, in his history of twentieth-century painting, summarizes his career in these words:

> For many years Villon had completely abandoned painting, then shortly before and during the war he went back to his original manner, which he fashioned into an instrument for the lyrical and musical interpretation of the world of objects. His new work, shown after the war, appealed greatly to many young painters by its poetic hermeticism, which corresponded to their own aims, and soon his name was on everyone's lips. Villon's method consists in transforming natural light into a hovering, somewhat honey-colored light, and then consolidating the luminous structure by means of delicate geometric pattern, so that the colored light forms crystals. The natural motif is

refracted in this rigorously geometrical structure as in a prism and within the subtly regulated pattern takes on a magical transparency which enables it to shine forth from the pictorial ground as lyrical reflection of reality.[11]

Like Bonnard, whom Villon loved above all other contemporary painters and who he felt had not received his due, the artist produced his finest work at the very end of his life. At this time, in his eighties, he was honored with large retrospectives in Paris and New York, and museums and private collectors vied with each other to acquire his outstanding canvases, most of which were produced in his old age, for it was only in his seventies and eighties that he had fully realized his very personal artistic vision. He continued working to the end of his long and immensely creative life and died in 1963, shortly before his eighty-eighth birthday, universally hailed as one of the true masters of modern French painting. His canvases now hang next to those of his great contemporaries in the leading museums of the world.

Somewhat younger than these artists was the German painter Julius Bissier, whose artistic career is probably the most amazing demonstration of how a painter who has received very little recognition during most of his life can emerge dramatically as a widely recognized artist in his old age. Born in Freiburg im Breisgau in 1893, the early years of Bissier's life were spent in the study of art history and painting, followed by service as a soldier in the German army during the First World War. Perhaps the most significant event of these early years was his friendship with the art historian Ernst Grosse, who introduced him to Far Eastern art and thought, which were to have a lasting influence on him. His first success came when he won prizes in Düsseldorf and Hanover for some rather conventional realistic paintings and he was appointed professor at the university in his native city. By 1929, the artist was turning increasingly toward abstraction, a tendency accentuated by meeting Brancusi in

[11] Werner Haftmann, *Painting in the Twentieth Century*, vol. 1 (New York: Praeger, 1966), p. 332.

Paris in 1930. However, the advent of the Hitler regime and the complete destruction of his studio during a fire in 1934 proved disastrous for his artistic career, and at the outbreak of the Second World War in 1939, Bissier, now forty-seven, moved to the small village of Hagnau at Lake Constance. It was here that he lived most of his remaining years, with the final years spent in Ascona.

It was at Lake Constance, living far from any art center in a country at war whose official policy forbade the making of abstract art, that Bissier evolved into a highly original painter. Starting with colored monotypes in 1947 and abstract ink paintings reminiscent of Japanese calligraphy, he slowly developed a style of his own that combined the spirituality of the East with the sensibility of modern abstract art. In 1953, his sixtieth year, he began painting in oil-tempera, and three years later he started the series of miniature paintings in this medium that were to bring him almost instant recognition as one of the finest and most original painters to have come out of postwar Germany. From this time on, one exhibition of his work followed another, starting with the participation in the Venice Biennale of 1958, a large retrospective organized by the Kestner Gesellschaft in Hanover in 1959, which traveled to several

*Julius Bissier*
*12 Dez 61 Aquarell*
*1961*
*Courtesy LeFebre Gallery, New York*

*Julius Bissier went unrecognized as an artist until after his sixtieth year. This work was painted in 1961, when Bissier was sixty-eight.*

other German cities, and other comprehensive exhibitions in Brussels, Zurich, the Hague, London, and New York. After a lifetime of neglect, Bissier, now almost seventy, was showered with awards and honors not only in his native country but also abroad. Yet strangely enough, the artist's reaction to all this late success was not joy but a feeling that the fates would revenge themselves, and indeed they did, for he died shortly after, in 1965, at the age of seventy-two.

These late works on which the artist's reputation rests have often been compared to Klee's, probably because both painters liked to work in watercolor and to use a small format, but as Bissier said, "There is no comparing Paul Klee's work with my symbols."[12] He is actually far closer to the great Chinese and Japanese ink painters, especially those of the Zen school. It was not pure chance that he was interested in Eastern mysticism and belonged to an artists' society that called itself the Zen group.[13] Like the Oriental masters, he tried to transcend mere visual reality and create what he called life signs, symbols of the ultimate reality. Using very simple, abstract forms and representing objects such as vases, bottles, fruits, plants, and plus and minus signs, the artist created what he called a dialogue with nature. Through them he bore witness to a vision going far beyond the ordinary and he did so with a mastery and sensibility that surpassed that of any other modern German painter.

Another contemporary artist whose outstanding contribution to modern art was made during his later years is Richard Lindner. Born in Hamburg in 1901 and growing up in Bavaria, he originally wanted to become a musician, but in 1922 he turned to the visual arts, studying first in Nuremberg and then at the Academy of Fine Arts in Munich. After this he was employed by a publishing house as an art adviser but being Jewish was forced to leave his native country after Hitler's rise to power in 1933. He went first to Paris, where he spent a few years and met Picasso and Gertrude Stein, and finally to the United States in 1941. In America he became a suc-

---

[12] T. Messer, *Julius Bissier* (San Francisco: Museum of Art, 1968), p. 41.
[13] Hugo Munsterberg, *Zen and Oriental Art* (Tokyo, and Rutland, Vt.: Charles E. Tuttle, 1965), p. 144.

cessful illustrator, working for such magazines as *Fortune*, *Vogue*, and *Harper's Bazaar*, and also achieving some success as a book illustrator. However, making his living by what he called "art by assignment" became increasingly distasteful to him and, encouraged by friends, he decided to give up commercial art in 1951, when he was fifty years old, and devote himself to painting.

In order to support his family, he took a modest job as an instructor at the Pratt Institute in Brooklyn. It was in this period that his career as a true artist began. Although he turned to full-time painting late in life, his imagery and style emerged almost full-grown. A first major work entitled *The Meeting*, painted in 1953 and now in The Museum of Modern Art in New York, already showed all the ingredients that were to characterize his art. In the following year he had his first one-man show at the Betty Parsons Gallery, which established his reputation as a highly original artist. In this early work it was Léger, with his mechanical rendering of man, who influences him most, as well as Duchamp, Picabia, and the Dadaists. He was also very interested in American popular culture as reflected in films and television. Interspersed with these artistic influences were the memories of his Bavarian childhood, with mad King Ludwig, among others, appearing in his canvases.

While these pictures showed great promise, it was only in 1961, when he was sixty years old, that his mature style evolved and Lindner became a truly important artist. No doubt this was partially due to the emergence of Pop art during the sixties as well as the return to a more figurative type of art that was congenial to him, but it is also true that his compositions became clearer and simpler and his imagery more lucid. His forms recall in some ways the magic realism of the German painters of the 1920s, such as Dix and Grosz, in the precision of his detail; they also suggest the toys of Nuremberg in their mechanical quality. These images of erotic women with voluptuous but strangely metallic forms have a haunting quality that impresses itself strongly on the viewer. Yet all of this is transformed by his American experience and contemporary Pop culture, for Lindner is the supreme artist of the world of Broadway and Forty-second Street, the world of prostitutes and pimps, gangsters and molls, the portrayer of the world of Coney Island and the cheap and tawdry amusement parks of the New York City area. As Dore

*Richard Lindner*
Ice
*1966*
*Courtesy Collection of Whitney*
*Museum of American Art,*
*Gift of the Friends of the Whitney*
*Museum of American Art,*
*New York*

*Richard Lindner's provocative*
*work* Ice *was painted in 1966*
*when the artist was sixty-five*
*years old.*

Ashton says in her book on the artist, "New York as a theme puts in its appearance tentatively in the late 1950s. By 1961, it is more insistent. We find the carnival barker transformed, in an early version of Coney Island, for instance, into an American gangster stereotype, with evil mustache, flashy suit, and slightly out of date air. The same is true of his new Lulu. Lulu's progress is fast in these years. In *The Walk* she is a gauntleted whore of rather metallic distinction. She dominates the picture plane. . . . She is the American whore, the New York whore."[14] And having developed his peculiar version of Pop realism, Lindner, now in his sixties and seventies, in a wealth of canvases and prints, gave expression to his vision of the tawdry and often repulsive but always fascinating American girl, displaying her erotic charms, sucking an ice-cream cone in a suggestive way, wearing provocative clothes and leather boots, enticing robots from a world closer to *Clockwork Orange* and *Lolita* than the traditional femme fatale of nineteenth-century painting and novels. He died, aged seventy-seven, in 1978.

[14] Dore Ashton, *Richard Lindner* (New York: Abrams, 1969), p. 49.

Among the sculptors who came into prominence only during their later years, by far the most remarkable is Louise Nevelson. Born in Kiev, Russia, in 1899 of a Jewish family that emigrated to America in 1905, the young Louise Berliavsky grew up in Maine. Although she early decided to become an artist, she first took up painting, studying at the Art Students League in New York and with Hans Hofmann in Munich. She also for a time served as an assistant of Diego Rivera and taught at the Educational Alliance School of Art. However, it was sculpture that was her main love and in 1941, when she was forty-two years old, she had her first one-man show at the Nierendorf Gallery in New York. Profoundly influenced by Cubism and primitive art, especially African and pre-Colombian carvings, she developed a distinctive style that reached its maturity during the 1950s when she was a woman in her fifties.

The culmination came in 1959, in her sixtieth year, with her exhibition called "Moon Garden and One" at the Grand Central Modern Gallery in New York, whose director, Colette Roberts, had been an early admirer of the artist and had already given her shows in 1955 and 1956. The same year she was included in The Museum of Modern Art's "Sixteen American Artists" show, and from then on her position as one of the most eminent American sculptors was assured. In 1962 her work was shown at the American pavilion at the Venice Biennale, and in 1965 she was the first woman artist and first sculptor given a one-man show at the Sidney Janis Gallery. She was also elected president of the National Artists Equity, and in 1967, the Whitney Museum of American Art honored her with a large retrospective.

Working in a style all her own, Nevelson in old age has created and is still busy creating a body of work that surpasses that of any of her younger contemporaries. As she once said, "I don't think an 'artist' has a right to that title much until he finds a unique, a private way of making his statement."[15] Using crates, pieces of furniture, and ornamental elements of old buildings, she assembles architectural constructions of great beauty and power. Usually painting

[15] Louise Nevelson in *Current Biography*, 1967, pp. 314–317.

them black, although at times she has also used white or gold, she creates out of them entire walls and environments that produce a mysterious and awe-inspiring quality. Names such as *Sky Cathedral* suggest religious overtones, and it may not be pure chance that her

*Louise Nevelson*
Expanding Reflection Zag II
*1977*
*Courtesy Collection Robert Ades*
*Photo Courtesy The Pace Gallery, New York*

*This recent work by Louise Nevelson,* Expanding Reflection Zag II, *was completed in 1977 when the artist was seventy-eight.*

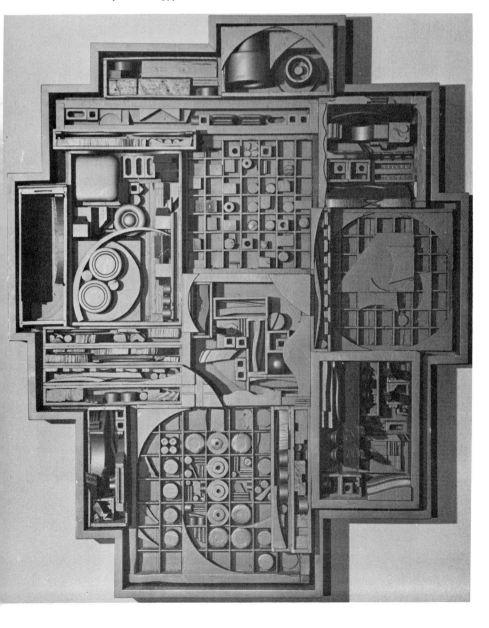

*Louise Nevelson*
Chapel of the Good Shepherd,
*1976*
*St. Peter's Lutheran Church, New York*
*Photo Courtesy The Pace Gallery*

*One of Louise Nevelson's most recent projects,* The Chapel of the
Good Shepherd *for St. Peter's Lutheran Church in New York, was
completed in 1976 when the artist was seventy-seven years old.*

most ambitious project of recent years is the creation of an entire
chapel, recalling Matisse's work of his old age in Vence, for St.
Peter's Lutheran Church in New York City. Designing not only the
altar and the cross but the vestments for the pastor, she has produced what may well prove to be the most unique and important
work of modern religious art in New York City.

Although over eighty, Louise Nevelson is at the very height
of her creative power, producing monumental sculptures such as the
one for the Wall Street district in New York and the large religious
work for Temple Israel in Boston as well as innumerable smaller
pieces made of wood, metal, Plexiglas, and plastic. Her output is not
only vast but on a very high artistic level, with her best creations
among the greatest of modern sculptures—as well as among the
finest works being made by any living woman artist.

She does not restrict herself to her chosen field but has also been working in the graphic arts. In 1964 she received a grant to go to the Tamarind Lithography Workshops in Los Angeles, and although already sixty-five at the time, with her usual energy and creativity she took to this art form, new to her, with great enthusiasm and made some of the finest prints produced in America in recent years. After decades of hardship and struggle during which she received little recognition or encouragement, Nevelson has now, in her eighties, emerged as one of the truly great artists of our age and is showered with honors and commissions. Far from being overwhelmed by this development, she accepts it as her due and continues to produce a wealth of masterpieces.

Turning next to architecture, an outstanding example of a leading figure in this field who did his most significant work in his later years is Louis Kahn. He was born in 1901 on the island of Osel off the coast of Estonia, at that time a part of Czarist Russia. His parents, like Louise Nevelson's, left Russia after the great pogrom of 1905, came to America, and settled in Philadelphia, where Kahn grew up and spent most of his life. He received his training as an architect at the University of Pennsylvania in the prevailing Beaux Arts tradition. Following this, he worked as a draftsman and designer in various architectural offices and traveled in Europe, studying the great monuments of Medieval and Renaissance architecture. In keeping with the spirit of the 1930s, he was particularly interested in urban planning and housing and in 1937, at the age of thirty-six, became consultant architect for the Philadelphia Housing Authority and two years later served in the same capacity for the U.S. Housing Authority.

In addition to his activities as a builder, he also became an influential teacher, first as a professor of architecture at Yale from 1947 to 1957; and after that he taught at his alma mater, the University of Pennsylvania. In fact, during his earlier years his influence as a stimulating teacher was far greater than his influence as an architect, for he was well over fifty when he began to design the structures for which he became famous. The 1940s, dominated by the exponents of the International style, notably Mies van der Rohe and

Walter Gropius, apparently were not conducive to the unfolding of Kahn's particular architectural vision outside of the classroom, where he was able to develop his artistic ideas.

The first building in which he was able truly to express himself was the design for the new Yale University Art Gallery, which he built in conjunction with Douglas Orr between 1951 and 1953, when he was in his early fifties. But it was not until the end of this decade, when Kahn was almost sixty, that he was recognized as one of the great masters of modern architecture for his design of the Richards Medical Research Building of the University of Pennsylvania. This structure, which was erected between 1957 and 1961, has been described as perhaps the clearest statement of Kahn's philosophy. It was at once recognized as a major work of art and was honored with a one-building show at The Museum of Modern Art. The Museum *Bulletin* described it as ". . . probably the single most consequential building constructed in the U.S. since the war." Ada Louise Huxtable, writing in *The New York Times*, characterized the structure as "strong and meaningful . . . strikingly handsome, reaching beyond mere graciousness or elegance for fundamental architectural value."

OPPOSITE PAGE:
*Louis Kahn*
*Kimbell Art Museum*
*Exterior*
*1974*
*Photo Courtesy Kimbell Art Museum,*
*Fort Worth, Texas*

*The Kimbell Art Museum in Fort*
*Worth, Texas, was the last design Louis*
*Kahn completed before his death in*
*1974 at the age of seventy-three.*

*Louis Kahn*
*Kimbell Art Museum*
*Interior*
*1974*
*Photo Courtesy Kimbell Art Museum,*
*Fort Worth, Texas*

*This building was designed when the*
*architect was seventy-three.*

With this building Kahn emerged almost overnight as the spokesman for the new post-Bauhaus architecture. He has been called "The prophet of the suppressed generation: the ideas he truly held could not have developed or been put into convincing practice during the period 1925–1960 because of the unfavorable (not to say totalitarian) aesthetic climate. This is suggested by the facts of Kahn's life and the character of his work. Up to the age of fifty-five we see him designing à contre-coeur, trying to make the best of a palette of materials, techniques and programs which are foreign to his true purposes. After fifty-five we see him suddenly put into a position to do his thing."[16]

Combining as he did the lessons of the past with the technological developments of the present, Kahn achieved a great deal during the remaining years of his life and became one of the most sought after and influential architects. In his finest buildings there are a strength and elegance, a feeling of mass, and a beauty of materials and surface that are truly remarkable. His achievement was hailed

[16] Romaldo Giurgola and Jaimini Mehta, *Louis Kahn* (Boulder, Colo.: Westview Press, 1975), p. 32.

not only in the United States but also abroad. In 1971, on the occasion of his seventieth birthday, the American Institute of Architects awarded him their Gold Medal, and in the following year the Royal Institute of British Architects did likewise.

Of his later works, the finest is perhaps the design for the Jonas Salk Institute of Biological Studies at La Jolla, California, which dates from 1959 to 1965. It is particularly successful in its blending of the building with the landscape setting, for to Kahn, man, nature, and structure appeared as equal components that should be related to each other. Salk, who had much admired the Richards tower in Philadelphia, had chosen Kahn as the one architect he wanted for his Institute, and this choice proved a wise one, for it results in one of the great masterpieces of twentieth-century architecture, combining as it does utility with beauty and modernity with timelessness, reflecting, as Vincent Scully said in his book on Kahn, "patterns from Rome and most particularly, from Ancient Rome as imaged by Piranesi."[17]

This work is only one of the many outstanding structures Kahn built during his sixties and early seventies, which for him was an immensely creative decade. All kinds of buildings were designed by him during this period, churches such as the Unitarian Church in Rochester, New York, a theater in Fort Wayne, Indiana, an art Museum in Fort Worth, Texas, a library and dining hall for Exeter Academy in New Hampshire, a factory for Olivetti in Harrisburg, Pennsylvania, and a temple in Chappaqua, New York. Of his foreign projects, the most important is probably the Indian Institute of Management in Ahmedabad, which was built in 1963. He designed other buildings in Dacca in Bangladesh, in Venice, and in Jerusalem. A few months before his death, Kahn was asked to plan, together with the Japanese architect Tange, a new Institutional and Commercial Center in Teheran. His last design was a landscape composition created as a memorial to Franklin Delano Roosevelt on Roosevelt Island in New York City, but before it could be completed, Louis Kahn died at the age of seventy-three in 1974.

[17] Vincent Scully, *Louis I. Kahn* (New York: Braziller, 1962), p. 37.

# 3 NEVER TOO LATE TO BEGIN

*I*t is very rare indeed for those who take up art for the first time in their old age to achieve any degree of eminence. However, there are a few gifted persons who achieve true excellence after starting to paint or sculpt in their later years. In the Western world they are usually the so-called primitives, since they lack the kind of academic training that a successful career in the arts usually demands. In spite of this, the best of them can become outstanding artists who, within the framework of these limitations, produce works of originality and charm. In the Far East this phenomenon of taking up painting in one's old age after retirement from work as a government official or a businessman is very common. Since those who do this usually belong to the class of the educated people, who are deeply steeped in painting and calligraphy, they do not suffer from the limitations of their Western colleagues and are able to achieve the highest levels of artistic attainment. In fact, some of them are among the greatest of Chinese and Japanese painters.

The most remarkable of these modern primitives is Anna Mary Robertson Moses, who achieved world fame under the name of Grandma Moses. Born in Greenwich, New York, in 1860, she died at the age of one hundred and one in 1961. She had a long and very productive life as the wife of a farmer in upstate New York, raising her large family and taking care of the house. A true primitive, Grandma Moses had never received any painting lessons or taken any serious interest in art until late in life, although she had done some painting and decorating around the house. But after her husband's death in 1927, when she was sixty-seven years old and her youngest son and his wife took over the farm, she began creating pictorial designs, first in worsted embroidery and later in colors on canvas, in order to have something to do. Initially she thought of painting merely as an occupation to keep her busy, something to pass the time away, since she was suffering from neuritis and arthritis and could do little work around the farm. As she said, "It is a very pleasant hobby if one does not have to hurry. I love to take my time and finish things up right. At first I painted for pleasure, then I was called upon to do more than I could, to live up to my promises."[1]

Grandma Moses was probably well over seventy when she took up painting, but she exhibited at once an artistic creativity and feeling for color and design that is extraordinary. Painting her own world, the house in which she lived, the life of the farm, the countryside of upstate New York, the local fairs and family celebrations, she brought to these scenes a vividness and joy of life that gives her pictures the appeal and interest that they were at once felt to have. Her works, in fact, have a naïve charm, which only the paintings of a very few of the modern primitives possess. At the same time, unlike most of them, Grandma Moses also had a fine sense of color and pattern, which make her paintings visually very rewarding. As a result, her work achieved national and even international success after being discovered by Louis Caldor, a New Jersey collector, who saw one of her pictures in a drugstore in Hoosick Falls in 1938.

[1] Otto Kallir, *Grandma Moses* (New York: Abrams, 1973), p. 269.

*Grandma Moses*
Black Horses
*1942*
*Courtesy Collection Otto Kallir,*
*Copyright Grandma Moses Properties, Inc., New York*

*This painting was executed when the artist was eighty-two years old.*

Because of his enthusiasm she was included in the 1938 Modern Primitives exhibition at The Museum of Modern Art in New York devoted to Contemporary Unknown American Painting. She has also been shown regularly since 1940 in the St. Etienne Gallery in New York, which is run by her friend and admirer, Otto Kallir. A critic, reviewing her first show at this establishment, referred to her as Grandma Moses, a name that has stuck with her ever since.

A prolific artist, she painted well over a thousand pictures during her lifetime, although she took up art only in her seventies and her first comprehensive exhibition was held when she was eighty. However, she continued working to the very end of her life. Her last canvas was painted shortly before her death, when she was over one hundred years old. Her appeal was very wide not only in the United States but also in Vienna, Munich, the Hague, Paris, and Moscow. Wherever Grandma Moses was shown, her work was greeted with great warmth and enthusiasm. In 1948 she was received in the

White House by President Truman, and in 1950 a film was made about her, narrated by the famous poet Archibald MacLeish. Depicting the older and simpler America of her youth in a detailed and realistic style and in a "pleasing and cheerful manner," as she called it, her work is filled with nostalgia for a rural and small-town life that evokes happy memories. At the same time she is, in her somewhat primitive and untaught way, a true artist manipulating her forms, patterns, and colors with great aesthetic sensitivity and achieving, at her best, remarkable results.

Among the male self-taught painters in the United States, the most outstanding was Morris Hirshfield. He was born into a Polish-Jewish family in Russia in 1872. At the age of eighteen, he emigrated to America and found a position in a women's coat factory. After several years of hard work, he was able to form his own company with his brothers, first manufacturing women's coats and suits and later slippers, a field in which he proved successful. Although he had already shown some artistic gifts as a child, it was not until he retired from the textile business at the age of sixty-five in 1937 that he began painting seriously. Talking about his first pictures in an autobiographical sketch, he said,

> My first paintings, on which I worked so laboriously and which took me so long to produce, were started in 1937 and were called the *Beach Girl* and *Angora Cat*. It seems that my mind knew well what I wanted to portray but my hands were unable to produce what my mind demanded. After working five months on one and then on the other in 1937, I could not carry them out to my satisfaction and put them to one side, coming back again to them in 1938, when once again, I worked on them for about five or six months. While they were very much improved, they still did not satisfy me and so again I put them to one side. It was when I took them up again in 1939 for the third time that I brought them out to my entire satisfaction.[2]

[2] Sidney Janis, *They Taught Themselves* (New York: The Dial Press, 1942), p. 18.

Morris Hirschfield
Girl in a Mirror
*1940*
*Courtesy Collection,*
*The Museum of Modern Art,*
*New York*

*Hirschfield did not begin to paint until late in life.*
Girl in a Mirror *was painted in 1940 when the*
*artist was sixty-eight.*

After this slow beginning Hirshfield, although never receiving any formal training, developed into an accomplished and productive artist who spent the remaining years of his life dedicated to his painting. Executed in a very detailed, meticulous manner in a genuinely primitive style, they have a childlike charm and naïveté that is delightful. Sidney Janis was the first to discover him, and he was shown in the exhibition of Modern Primitives at The Museum of Modern Art, and collectors almost at once began buying his work. Paintings such as *Girl in a Mirror* and *Nude at the Window* with their latent eroticism, painted when he was almost seventy, and the somewhat earlier *Lion and a Tiger* show him at his best. He died at the age of seventy-four in 1946.

While the two leading modern primitive painters in America were an Anglo-Scottish farm wife and an immigrant Jewish tailor, the leading self-taught sculptor was a southern Negro whose parents had been slaves in Tennessee. His name was William Edmundson and he was born in Nashville around 1880, the exact date not being known. His death certificate gives his age as sixty-eight in 1951, but it is probably merely an approximation. As a young man, he worked for the Nashville, Chattanooga and St. Louis Railway, but after an accident in 1907, he had to give up this type of work and he became a handyman in a women's hospital, where he worked for some twenty-five years until it closed in 1931. After this he simply "piddled around in the garden" and did odd jobs in the neighborhood. It was during this period of his life, when he was already in his fifties, that he for the first time, as he put it, "cut away on some stones."

As Edmundson saw it, it was God who was telling him to take up sculpture, for he said, "I knowed it was God telling me what to do. God was telling me to cut figures. First He told me to make tomb stones; then He told me to cut out figures. He gave me them two things."[3] Working largely in limestone in a very simple, direct style, he produced carvings that had a naïve and strong beauty all their own. Although he did not consider himself an artist but only a person who was just doing the "Lord's Work," his gifts were soon recognized by the good offices of the Nashville collectors, the Starrs, and the photographer Louise Dahl-Wolfe. In 1937, when the artist was probably around sixty, he was given a one-man show at The Museum of Modern Art, and in 1938 he was included in an exhibition called "Three Centuries of Art in the United States," which was held in Paris. For the next ten years he produced a large body of work representing animals and figures that combined a fine sense of the material with a mystic vision that brought his images to life. His sudden success astonished him and especially his neighbors, who had known him as a simple laborer, but as he saw it, it was God who was

[3] Edmond L. Fuller, *Visions in Stone, The Sculptures of William Edmundson* (Pittsburgh: University of Pittsburgh Press, 1973), p. 8.

telling him to create these works and it was this inner voice that he was following. By the end of the 1940s, when he was nearing seventy, his health began to decline and he was unable to continue his carving. He died on February 7, 1951.

Among the French naïve artists who took up painting in their advanced years, the most remarkable was Louis Vivin. He was born in the small village of Hadol near Epinal in the Vosges region in 1861 and died in the Montmartre district of Paris in 1936 at the age of seventy-five. From childhood on he had been passionately fond of drawing but was not able to pursue art seriously until after his retirement from the postal service in 1922. He spent most of his life working for the Paris central post office, first as a letter carrier, then a chief clerk, and finally as an inspector. During this period he made a large map of France, on which he carefully marked all post offices; this earned him the congratulations of his superiors and an Academy award.

Although he had done some painting as a hobby in his earlier years, it was not until he was sixty that he could devote himself to it full time, and he was seventy before he became well known as an artist. Prior to that he had sold his work to the passersby in the marketplace of Sacre-Coeur for a few francs each. He lived quite apart from the art world, ". . . knew none of the artists of his time, never set foot in an exhibition, never read a single piece of art criticism."[4] A true primitive, he used a meticulously realistic style, building up his compositions out of many carefully rendered small forms, like a child constructing a house out of many small blocks. With tremendous care, each brick and stone of a façade, each leaf and branch of a tree were rendered with great precision in order to get the most accurate and complete picture of the visual reality. The result was a kind of magic realism or even a Surrealistic effect that has a fascination all its own. Although he often worked from postcards and admired Meissonier above all other painters, his depictions of Montmartre and the streets and places of Paris and other

[4] Catalog of "Masters of Popular Painting" (New York: The Museum of Modern Art, 1938), p. 47.

*Louis Vivin*
Church of St. Laurent and the Gare de l'Est
*c. 1922–1936*
*(no longer extant)*
*Courtesy Collection, The Museum of Modern Art, New York*

*The French primitive painter Vivin produced works like* Church
of St. Laurent and the Gare de l'Est *from his retirement in 1922
at sixty until his death in 1936.*

cities have an eerie quality in which tiny human beings seem to be
inhabiting a strange and haunting urban landscape created out of
the artist's own imagination.

In England the most outstanding of the modern primitives was
Alfred Wallis, who was born in Devonport in 1855 and died in 1942
in St. Ives in Cornwall at the age of seventy-seven. As a youth, he
had gone to sea and worked as a fisherman, but in 1890, at the age
of forty-five, he opened a junk shop for sailors in St. Ives, which
gave him the nickname "Old Iron" by which he became known.[5] In
1875 he married a widow with seventeen children who was twenty-

[5] K. H. Olbricht, *Old Iron, der Maler von St. Ives, Die Kunst und das Schöne Heim,*
December 1975, pp. 726–728.

one years older than he, and it was only after her death in 1922, when he was sixty-seven, that he took up painting to overcome the loneliness he felt without her company. He was in his seventies when two leading modern English painters, Christopher Wood and Ben Nicholson, discovered his work in 1928 and included him as a Cornish primitive in their group exhibitions.

The subjects Wallis depicted, largely taken from his days as a sailor, were mostly ships, harbors, coastal areas, and seascapes executed in a truly primitive, very awkward manner with little understanding of perspective, space, or atmosphere. At the same time he was a true artist who had a fine sense of design and color and used crude but bold brushstrokes. Although completely self-taught, Wallis from the very start showed great artistic sensitivity so

*Alfred Wallis*
Schooner under the Moon
*c. 1935–1936*
*Courtesy The Tate Gallery, London*

> *Alfred Wallis, a British primitive painter whose imaginative work has a naïve charm, painted* Schooner under the Moon *in 1936 when he was eighty-one years old.*

that he even influenced Wood and Nicholson for a time. As Wood wrote to a friend, "I am more and more influenced by Alfred Wallis —not a bad master though he and Picasso both mix their colors on box lids. I see him each day for a second—he is bright and cheery. I'm not surprised that nobody likes Wallis' paintings; no one liked Van Gogh's for a long time, did they?"[6] While the last comparison may be somewhat exaggerated, it is nevertheless true that Wallis's work has gained the respect of the artistic community, and today he is regarded as a leading British primitive painter whose work has a naïve charm and great imaginative power.

In Japan, where the tradition of amateur painters in the best sense of the term is a very old one, the phenomenon of a person's beginning an artistic career after retirement is quite common, and some of the greatest Japanese masters fall into this category. Outstanding among them was Uragami Gyokudo, who lived from 1745 to 1820. Born into an ancient samurai family, he served the lord Ikeda Masaka of Bizen for many years and had the opportunity to visit Edo, the present-day Tokyo, which was the seat of the Tokugawa shoguns. A man of culture, he studied music, especially the koto, painting, calligraphy, poetry, and the Chinese classics. At the death of his lord in 1794, he gave up his official position and devoted himself wholly to music and art. Wandering about the countryside, drinking sake with friends, playing music, Gyokudo led the life of a free spirit who, after years of service, enjoyed pursuing his own interests. In 1798, now fifty-three years old, he settled in Kyoto and became a member of a circle of literati painters among whom were the two most famous Nanga painters of the time, Aoki Mokubei and Tano-mura Chikuden.

It was only at this point that Gyokudo seriously turned to painting, a field in which up to that time he was a mere amateur. As a recent book on Nanga painting says, "Gyokudo's painting was self-taught. He produced little before his resignation, and most of his work was done after that event, the most characteristic after he

---

[6] John Rothenstein, *Modern English Painters*, vol. 2 (New York: St. Martin's Press, 1974), p. 21.

was past sixty. The later paintings are frankly expressive of his innermost feelings, revealing his melancholia and even, sometimes, his utter rage."[7] Having been deeply steeped in traditional Japanese and Chinese ink painting and calligraphy, he could of course draw upon his background in developing his own style, so that there can be no comparison between such a Japanese scholar-painter and an American or European person who, after pursuing a career as an official, decides to devote himself to painting in his old age.

Gyokudo, far from remaining a mere dilettante, is considered by many modern critics, both Japanese and Western, one of the true giants of Japanese painting. Among artists of the Nanga or Southern school, which modeled itself on the Chinese painters of the literati tradition, he is considered second only to Ike-no-Taiga, and he is widely regarded as the last great master of the traditional Japanese painting of the Edo period. Modern critics, especially, have exhibited a great fondness for his eccentric genius, for as James Cahill says, "Gyokudo's paintings appeal powerfully to the twentieth-century eye and sensibility because, like the works of some Chinese individualist painters, with which they have strong affinities, they are satisfying and exciting in two ways: as pure form, in their ink and paper existence, and as profoundly moving visions of nature."[8]

His mature work, painted when he was in his sixties and seventies, interprets the landscape in a highly individual and expressive style similar to that employed by the Chinese Eccentric painters with whose pictures he must have been familiar. Using bold brushstrokes, sometimes applied in several layers, he achieved remarkably powerful and dramatic pictorial effects, sometimes resembling modern Expressionist painting. His theme, always the favorite one of the literati painters, is that of the grandeur and majesty of nature and the tiny figure of the sage wandering through the landscape or sitting in a small hut contemplating the mountains or reading a book. Titles such as *Idle in the Mountain, Two Peaks Embracing Clouds, Streams and Roads in a Deep, Damp Valley,* and *A Myriad of Sounds and Thousand-layered Peaks* are indicative of the kind of

---

[7] Yoshiho Yonezawa and Chu Yoshizawa, *Japanese Painting in the Literati Style* (Tokyo: Heibonsha Publishers, 1974), p. 89.
[8] James Cahill, *Scholar Painters of Japan: The Nanga School* (New York: Asia Society, 1972), p. 71.

*Uragami Gyokudo*
Sanchu Dankin
*c. 1810*
*Courtesy Freer Gallery of Art,*
*Smithsonian Institution,*
*Washington, D.C.*

Sanchu Dankin *is a late work*
*by Uragami Gyokudo, one of the*
*last great masters of traditional*
*Japanese painting of the Edo*
*period.*

subject he loved to paint, and it was in this realm that he produced
some of the most memorable scrolls ever to have come out of Japan.
After twenty years of producing a large number of such paintings,
he died at the age of seventy-five in 1820.


Another outstanding Japanese painter whose artistic career started
only in his old age was the Zen priest Sengai who lived from 1750 to
1837. He was a native of Mino province (the present Gifu prefec-
ture) and was trained at a Zen temple in his home district. After
eight years, he received permission to go to Toki-an near Yokohama
to study under the celebrated Zen master Gessen Zenji. At the con-

clusion of this period, he was invited to join the oldest of Japanese Zen temples, Shofukuji in Hakata, where he became the abbot in 1790. After his retirement from this position in 1811, when he was sixty-one, he took up painting and lived in Hakata as a lay monk. It was during these years that he developed into a great artist. Free from the cares of the world and no longer attached to a temple, he could now devote himself entirely to his art, and he became the finest religious painter of his time.

Sengai's output was vast, for he loved to paint rapidly in a few brushstrokes, employing an abstract ink style that at its best is truly inspired. However, since he painted such a large number of scrolls, the quality of his work is very uneven. His subjects varied, but he was particularly fond of Zen themes and figures from folklore, history, and legend, as well as landscapes and animals. A typical Zen

*Sengai*
Shoki
*c. 1820s*
*Collection Hugo Munsterberg,*
*New Paltz, New York*

*The Zen priest Sengai began painting late in life and became the finest religious painter of his time. Sengai's painting of a Shoki—Demon Queller—is thought to date from the 1820s, when the artist was in his seventies.*

painter, he used an artistic shorthand, saying profound things in a very simple way, often showing humor as he was doing so. His paintings were frequently accompanied by Zen sayings or crazy verses of his own making that allude to Zen parables and Chinese philosophy. His artistic activity continued with undiminished creativity to the time of his death in spite of the fact that he lived to an advanced old age, dying at eighty-seven in 1837. He was well known as a great Zen priest, an immensely productive and highly original painter, and an eccentric who was loved by all who came in contact with him.

# 4 THE WORK GOES ON...

$W$hile there are relatively few artists who did their best work in their late years or only started working when they were old, there are a great many who embarked upon an artistic career early in life and continued being active into old age, often up to the time of their death. Since there are so many of them, it would obviously be impossible to deal with their old-age work in any detail, so this discussion will be restricted to those who lived beyond a normal life-span and did significant work during the later years. Most of these reached their seventies or even eighties, but a few who made important contributions in their late sixties have also been included.

There can be little doubt that many of the great architects, sculptors, and painters of ancient times and the Medieval period reached old age and were able to continue their artistic production into their late years, but since little accurate information about their careers is available, the following discussion will be restricted to artists of the time beginning with the Renaissance and ending with the contemporary period. Emphasis is placed throughout upon the major figures in the various fields of artistic endeavor whose contribution in their old age is deemed important in terms of the history of art.

Of the great artists of the Italian Renaissance, the one who lived to be the oldest (aside from Michelangelo and Titian, who have already been discussed in an earlier chapter) and who did his finest work in his old age was Giovanni Bellini. Born in 1430 and dying in 1516, he lived to his eighty-sixth year and according to all accounts was vigorous and active to the very year of his death. Albrecht Dürer, who visited Venice in 1506, when Bellini was seventy-six, reported in a letter to his friend Pirkheimer that "He is very old and

*Giovanni Bellini*
The Feast of the Gods
*1513*
*Courtesy National Gallery of Art,*
*Washington, D.C.*

*Giovanni Bellini painted* The Feast of the Gods *in 1513 at the advanced age of eighty-three.*

still the best in painting,"[1] and upon hearing of the artist's death, Marino Sanudo wrote that although Bellini was very old he was still painting "most excellently." In fact it was during the last years of his life, starting in 1500, when he had reached his seventieth year, that the artist produced some of his greatest masterpieces. It is quite apparent that Bellini, even during his later years, was able to hold his own in relation to younger rivals.

Characteristic for this late period in his artistic career are the great altarpiece of the *Madonna Enthroned with Saints* at the Church of San Saccaria in Venice, which was painted in 1505 when the master was seventy-five, and the various pictures of Mary and the Christ Child, such as the lovely *Madonna of the Meadows* in the National Gallery in London, which is believed to have been painted around the turn of the century. But the most remarkable canvases of Bellini's old age, executed when he was in his eighties, were the large painting of *The Feast of the Gods* of 1513, now in the National Gallery in Washington, D.C., and the *Venus*, or *Lady at Her Toilet*, in the Kunsthistorische Museum in Vienna, which was painted only one year before his death and shows that Bellini in his mid-eighties was still in full control of his artistic genius.

Other Quattrocento painters who lived long and productive lives and did some of their finest work in their late years were Paolo Uccello, Andrea Mantegna, and Luca Signorelli, yet they are merely the most outstanding of the many artists who were still working in their seventies. The oldest of the three was Uccello, who was born in 1397 and died in 1475. A Florentine, he painted his most famous works, the three great battle scenes now in the Uffizi in Florence, the Louvre in Paris, and the National Gallery in London, for the Medici family between 1455 and 1460. In 1465, when he was sixty-eight, he moved to Urbino. It was here that he painted the predella representing the Profanation of the Host, which has been described "as the earliest depiction of a pogrom in Italian painting,"[2] and his last great masterpiece, *The Hunt at Night*, now in the Ashmolean Mu-

---

[1] Giles Robertson, *Giovanni Bellini* (Oxford: Oxford University Press, 1968), p. 1.
[2] H. Keller, *The Renaissance in Italy* (New York: Abrams, 1969), p. 76.

seum in Oxford, which is believed to have been painted around 1469. In that year he said, "I find myself old and ailing, my wife is ill and I can no longer work."[3] Six years later he died at the age of seventy-eight.

Mantegna, the leading painter of the Mantuan school, was born in Padua in 1431 and died at the age of seventy-five in 1506. Active as an artist to the very end of his life, he painted some of his most celebrated pictures during his late period. One of the best known is the *Judith and Holofernes* of 1495, painted when he was sixty-five, which is now in the National Gallery in Washington, D.C. But the most famous of his late works, now in the Louvre, are the pictures intended for the study of Isabella d'Este. They reflect his great interest in classical antiquity, for they represent Parnassus and Minerva Expelling the Vices from the Grove of Virtue. These compositions, painted around his seventieth year, show the artist at the very height of his power, combining in a most effective way the classical and humanistic with the naturalistic tendencies of the Renaissance.

[3] Enzo Carli, *All the Paintings of Paolo Uccello* (New York: Hawthorn, 1963), p. 46.

*Andrea Mantegna*
Judith and Holofernes
*1495*
*Courtesy National Gallery of Art,*
*Widener Collection,*
*Washington, D.C.*

Judith and Holofernes *is a late*
*work by Andrea Mantegna, leading*
*painter of the Mantuan School, and*
*was completed in 1495 when the*
*artist was in his sixty-fifth year.*

However, these pictures are but a few of the many fine paintings Mantegna produced during his old age.

The other Italian painter of this period who reached an advanced age was Signorelli. There is some disagreement about the date of his birth, with some authorities claiming that he was born in 1441 and others believing that his birth took place in 1450; but since he died in 1523, he was at least in his seventies and probably in his eighties at the time of his death. His most ambitious and influential works were the frescoes at the cathedral of Orvieto, which he painted between 1499 and 1506 when he was around sixty. His treatment of the Damned and the Resurrection of the Flesh in this cycle, with the

*Luca Signorelli*
Calvary
*1505*
*Courtesy National Gallery of Art,*
*Samuel H. Kress Collection, Washington, D.C.*

*Luca Signorelli is believed to have been in his sixties when he painted* Calvary.

angels blowing trumpets and the dead rising from their graves, is especially impressive and is believed to have influenced Michelangelo. Although never reaching these heights again, Signorelli continued working, producing among other fine works a series of small panels for the Palazzo Pandofo Petrucchi in Siena between 1505 and 1513, and religious paintings like the *Calvary* of 1505, now in the National Gallery in Washington, D.C.

In northern Europe, the outstanding Renaissance painter who reached a ripe old age was Lucas Cranach, who lived to be eighty-one. He was born in 1472 and died in 1553. A prolific artist who, together with his workshop, produced a large body of work, he continued painting well into his seventies, although it is often not certain if some of his very late pictures were executed by his own hand. In any case, he remained active to the very end of his life, not only as an artist but also as a citizen of his adopted city of Wittenberg, where he served three rulers of Saxony as court painter. In 1537, at the age of sixty-five, he was elected burgomaster of the town, and three years later he was reelected for another term. His portraits of the elector John Frederick, who was his patron, and especially of Martin Luther and Philipp Melanchthon, the great leaders of the Protestant Reformation, are among his best late pictures. Equally fine are his numerous depictions of the Virgin, as well as his charming nude Venuses, which are still indebted to the late Gothic tradition but already anticipate northern Mannerism.

Next to Michelangelo and Titian, the greatest Venetian painter of the sixteenth century was without question Tintoretto. His real name was Jacopo Robusti, and he was born in Venice in 1518 and died

*Lucas Cranach*
*Venus*
*1532*
*Courtesy Städelsches Kunstinstitut,*
*Frankfurt*

*Lucas Cranach the Elder*
*painted this charming Venus*
*in 1532 at the age of sixty.*

there at the age of seventy-six in 1594. An immensely vigorous man, he produced some of his greatest paintings during his old age and remained in full control of his powers to the time of his death. During his final year, he was still engaged in finishing his *Last Supper* and the *Gathering of Manna* for the Church of San Giorgio in Mantua, but it is upon his great cycle of paintings for the Scuola di San Rocco in Venice that his fame rests. This series of magnificent works was started in 1564, when he was only forty-six, but it was continued over a period of twenty-five years so that some of these pictures, notably those representing the Life of the Virgin in the Lower Hall, were painted during the 1580s, when he was a man in his late sixties. But, his largest and most ambitious painting, the *Paradise* in the Sala del Maggior Consiglio at the Ducal Palace in

*Tintoretto*
Bacchus and Ariadne
*1578*
*Ducal Palace, Venice*

*Tintoretto was sixty in 1578 when he completed this painting of* Bacchus and Ariadne *for the Ducal Palace in Venice.*

Venice, was painted in 1588, when he was already seventy. However, he had already painted some magnificent classical subjects for the Palazzo Ducale earlier.

It was during this late period that Tintoretto developed the mature manner in which he attenuates his figures and employs a sketchy brushwork that reduces the forms to light and color. In contrast to the naturalism of the Quattrocento and the Classicism of the High Renaissance, Tintoretto in these works evolves a new artistic style that is today usually referred to as Mannerist. There is in these pictures a new emphasis on expressive emotion in dealing with sacred subject matter that reflects the spirit of the Counter Reformation. There is also an impressionistic rendering of the figures and landscape that is highly original. This style was to have a profound influence on the work of the young El Greco and it prepared the way for the next great artistic movement, the Baroque.

In the field of sculpture, the most important Renaissance figures, next to Donatello and Michelangelo, were Lorenzo Ghiberti and Luca della Robbia. Ghiberti lived to be seventy-four, having been born in 1381 and dying in 1455. A goldsmith by training, he had won the competition to complete the doors of the Baptistry of San Giovanni in Florence. It was this great project that occupied him for most of his life, for it was not finished until 1452, when he was seventy-one years old. The third of the great gilded bronze doors, which were known as the "Doors of Paradise," was the product of his old age and represents the high point of his artistic career. It combines the devoutness of the late Gothic period with the innovative spirit of the Renaissance and represents one of the great artistic achievements of Quattrocento Italy.

Della Robbia was somewhat younger than Ghiberti, for he was born in 1400 and lived until 1482. He was a prolific artist who continued working until his death and had many assistants and followers. A huge number of sculptures have been attributed to him, many of which were no doubt the work of his nephew Andrea della Robbia. He in turn had sons who continued the tradition of glazed terra-cotta sculptures for which della Robbia is famous. Luca della Robbia's favorite subjects were the Madonna, done in blue and

*Luca della Robbia*
Adoration of the Magi
*c. 1472*
*Courtesy Victoria and Albert Museum, London*

*This work, the* Adoration of the Magi, *is attributed to Luca della Robbia and is*
*believed to have been executed in 1472 when the sculptor was seventy-two years old.*

white relief, and round portrait plaques. It is very difficult to date
them precisely, but there can be no doubt that some of the finest of
these come from his later years. This is particularly true of his last
major work at the Collegiata della Imprimata Tabernacle of the
Holy Cross with its representation of the Crucifixion, St. John, and
St. Augustine and Angels. The *Crucifixion with Mary and St. John*,
rendered in a very moving, dramatic manner, is regarded as one of
his greatest masterpieces, showing the artist at his very best in his old
age.

The dominant artistic figure of the Baroque period was Giovanni
Lorenzo Bernini, another of those fortunate persons who lived a
long and very creative life. Born in Naples in 1598, he spent most of
his life in Rome, where he died in 1680 at the age of eighty-two. He
was primarily a sculptor who could look back on a long and productive career by the time he was sixty, but he was also an important

architect, with most of his work in this field dating from the later years of his life. Outstanding among his buildings was the church of San Andrea al Quirinale in Rome, built between 1658 and 1670, between his sixtieth and seventy-second years. A small but beautiful edifice of oval design, it has a fine sculpture of St. Andrew, on whose image the movement of the lines converge, thus achieving a very dramatic effect. His architectural masterpiece is without doubt the large piazza in front of St. Peter's with its magnificent colonnade, a work begun in 1656 and completed in 1665, when the artist was sixty-seven years old.

Bernini also continued his work in sculpture and it was during the last two decades of his life that many of his finest carvings were made. Works such as the *St. Jerome* and *Mary Magdalene* in the Chigi Chapel in Siena, with their luminous expression and fervent religiosity, represent the very essence of the Baroque style and show the artist, a man in his sixties, at the very height of his power. His angels for San Andrea della Fratte in Rome are excellent manifesta-

*Giovanni Lorenzo Bernini*
*Piazza di San Pietro*
*1656–1665*
*Rome*

*An architect as well as a sculptor, Bernini created the beautiful Piazza di San Pietro during the years 1656–1665, his fifty-eighth to sixty-seventh years.*

tions of the spirit of the Counter Reformation. Particularly moving are the sculptures of his last decade, notably the *Blessed Lodovica Albertoni* in the Altieri Chapel of San Francesco a Ripa in Rome, made between 1671 and 1674. Here all the drama of the art of the Baroque finds its ultimate expression. Rudolf Wittkower, in writing about these late works, says, "The treatment of garments becomes increasingly impetuous, turbulent and sophisticated. They lose more and more the character of the real material and must be viewed as abstract patterns capable of conveying to the beholder a feeling of passionate spirituality."[4]

Equally impressive are the secular sculptures of his old age, notably those made for Louis XIV, who called him to Paris in 1665. Although nothing came of his plans to redesign the Louvre, his bust of the great ruler of France, now at Versailles, and his equestrian statue of the Sun King, which was executed between 1669 and 1677, between his seventy-first and seventy-ninth years, are among Bernini's masterpieces. He continued working in this area as well as in others to the time of his death and, as his son said in his biography of his father, "He succeeded in proving what he used to say, 'an artist excellent in design should not fear any want of vivacity or tenderness on reaching the age of decrepitude, because ability in design is so effective that it alone can make up for the defect of the spirits, which languish in old age.'"[5] When his death approached, he viewed it with equanimity, saying that ". . . that step was difficult for everyone because everyone took it for the first time."[6] He died of a stroke in 1680 at the age of eighty-two and was much lamented in Rome and throughout Europe.

There are many painters of this period who lived into their sixties and some who reached extreme old age. The two leading artists of the Dutch school, Rembrandt and Hals, have already been discussed. The famous Flemish painter Peter Paul Rubens died at sixty-

[4] Rudolf Wittkower, *Art and Architecture of Italy, 1600–1750* (Harmondsworth: Penguin, 1958), p. 99.
[5] D. Bernini, "The Life of the Cavalier Gian Lorenzo Bernini," quoted in *Bernini in Perspective*, ed. by George C. Bauer (Englewood, N.J.: Prentice-Hall, 1976), p. 37.
[6] Ibid., p. 39.

three, and his Spanish colleague Velázquez reached only sixty-one so that they are not included in this discussion of artists who worked in old age. The two leading French painters of the time, Nicolas Poussin and Claude Lorrain, lived to be seventy-one and eighty-two respectively, both of them active and productive artists to the end of their lives. In fact, it was their late work that in the eyes of most critics is considered their best, painted at an age that even by today's standards is considered old.

Poussin, who was the elder of the two great French seventeenth-century masters, was born in Normandy in 1594 and died in Rome in 1665. A lover of the ancients and the Italian Renaissance, he settled in the Eternal City in 1642. In contrast to Bernini and Rubens, who had exemplified the drama of the Baroque, Poussin strove for harmony and ideal beauty. He said: "My nature prompted me to search for order; confusion is foreign to me as excess." Working from nature and making detailed drawings of what he saw, he nevertheless superimposed upon it a sense of classical order and harmonious balance that give his paintings the serenity and beauty for which they are famous. This is particularly true of the pictures of his last decade when he reached his climax. As Walter Friedlaender observed,

> Aged artists seem to strive in their late works for totality of impression, and are less concerned with delineating details. Their works are frequently filled with new, moving lyricism that is a revival of their youthful style, but is a different, often elegiac tone that contrasts with the clear, more vigorous narrative or active expression in their mature work. These deficiencies and virtues of old age may be observed in the work of Nicolas Poussin. In his last years he was often ailing and in pain, and in a letter of the 1640s he already complains of his trembling hands . . . The old master was able to turn the insecurity of hand and his lines into an expressive factor of rare beauty.[7]

[7] Walter Friedlaender, *Nicolas Poussin—A New Approach* (New York: Abrams, 1964), p. 82.

*Nicolas Poussin*
Blind Orion Searching for the Rising Sun
*1658*
*Courtesy The Metropolitan Museum of Art,*
*Fletcher Fund, 1924, New York*

Blind Orion Searching for the Rising Sun, *painted in 1658 when Poussin was
sixty-four, is considered to be one of the artist's best late works.*

Turning increasingly to landscape painting or mythological
scenes with a landscape setting in which man's fragility is opposed to
the grandeur and endurance of nature, Poussin, now a man in his
sixties, produced his finest canvases. Pictures such as the *Blind
Orion Searching for the Rising Sun*, painted in 1658 and now in
The Metropolitan Museum of Art in New York, the *Landscape with
Two Nymphs and a Snake*, probably from the following year, and
his last works, the fantasy *Apollo and Daphne* and the *Four Seasons*, done from 1660 to 1664, in the Louvre, show the artist at his
very best. A man of seventy who was old and infirm, a lonely figure,
and a foreigner in a city where, according to him, "no friend can be
found," he nevertheless went on with his work. In 1665 he became
ill and died at the age of seventy-one.

His friend and countryman Claude Gelée, better known as Claude Lorrain since he was born near Nancy, the capital of ancient Lorraine, was six years younger than Poussin and survived him by seventeen years, living from 1600 to 1682. He too settled in Rome and devoted most of his life to the painting of landscapes and allegorical scenes taken from the writings of classical authors such as Virgil, whose *Aeneid* was one of his favorite subjects. His treatment of landscapes was very poetic, with the emphasis upon the lyrical aspects of nature. His forms were soft and modeled with a delicate use of tones and colors. Composing the mountains, trees, and rivers in carefully arranged groupings, he achieved a feeling of harmony and beauty that gives his canvases great appeal. A careful craftsman, he was wholly dedicated to his work and developed into an even more accomplished artist as he became older. As his biographer Sabine Cotte says, "Claude Lorrain's style reached its peak in his last works. His landscapes were sublime. Every element is perfectly balanced. . . . His handling of space is masterly . . . every picture presents a theme, a setting, a moment of time, brought together in a unique, precise relationship. The aim of Claude's late works was to tighten the relationship to the point of utmost harmony."[8] The pictures done when he was already a man in his seventies, such as the *Landscape with Hagar* and the *Angel* of 1668 in the National Gallery in London, *Apollo and the Muses on Mt. Parnassus* in The Metropolitan Museum in New York, and the *Noli Me Tangere* of 1681, executed when he was over eighty, are among his very finest works, indicating that Claude, as so many others, far from declining in his old age, continued to grow and evolved richer and more profound aesthetic effects. He died at eighty-two in 1682.

Among the architects of this period, the one who lived longest and contributed most in his old age was Sir Christopher Wren, who lived from 1632 to 1723. Originally a scientist, he had already had a

[8] Satine Cotte, *Claude Lorrain*, translated by H. Sebba (New York: Braziller, 1971), p. 59.

*Claude Lorrain*
Apollo and the Muses on Mount Parnassus
*1674*
*Courtesy The Metropolitan Museum of Art,*
*Rogers Fund, 1961, New York*

*Claude Lorrain at seventy-four was still producing such exceptional works as
his watercolor* Apollo and the Muses on Mount Parnassus, *dated 1674.*

brilliant career as a young man and become a professor of
astronomy at Oxford in 1661 and was one of the founders of the
Royal Society. Among his early architectural designs were the Shel-
donian Theatre at Oxford and the Library at Trinity College, Cambridge, but it was not until the Great Fire of London of 1666, at
which time the young architect was thirty-four, that he had the opportunity to show his true talents. In 1669 he was appointed
surveyor-general and was chosen chief architect for the new St.
Paul's and more than fifty other churches that had been destroyed by
the fire. In 1672 he was knighted, in 1680 he became president of
the Royal Society, and in 1698, at the age of sixty-six, he was appointed surveyor-general of Westminster Abbey.

Among the works that were produced in his old age, by far the
most impressive was St. Paul's Cathedral, which he envisaged as a

*Sir Christopher Wren*
*St. Paul's Cathedral*
*1675–1710*
*London*

*Sir Christopher Wren was*
*occupied with the design and*
*construction of St. Paul's*
*Cathedral for more than three*
*decades—from 1675 to 1710, his*
*forty-third to seventy-eighth*
*years.*

rival to St. Peter's. This great enterprise occupied him from 1675 to 1710, his fifty-third to his seventy-eighth years. The huge dome, which had presented particular problems, was in fact completed in only 1711, when he was almost eighty years old. Other good examples of the architecture of his old age are the Royal Hospital in Greenwich, which dates from 1698, and the Library at Queen's College, Cambridge, built between 1693 and 1696. Churches designed by Wren are found all over London, several of them dating from the late phase of his artistic career. They are usually two-story structures built of brick and dressed with stone, with a painted steeple over the tower. The style he employed was a rational and restrained one based on Palladian principles, for as Wren himself said, "Fancy blinds the judgment."[9] In 1714, when he was eighty-two years old, he was retired but was allowed to keep the title of

[9] K. Downes, *Christopher Wren* (London: Allen Lane, 1971), p. 21.

surveyor-general. He devoted the last years of his life to determining the accurate longitude. Wren died at the age of ninety-one and was buried in St. Paul's Cathedral, his masterpiece.

Although the first of the great eighteenth-century painters, Antoine Watteau, died prematurely at the age of thirty-seven, several other noteworthy painters of the time were blessed with long and productive lives. Outstanding among the French artists was Chardin. Jean Baptiste Simeon Chardin, who was born in Paris in 1699 and died there in 1779, was particularly fortunate, for not only was he able to remain active almost to his death at eighty but he was also greatly admired and sought after by his contemporaries. In fact, he was so highly esteemed that he was elected to the Royal Academy in 1728, and in 1757, at the age of fifty-eight, he was given an apartment in the Louvre. A superb craftsman whose artistic output was large and very even in quality, he nevertheless developed a richer and more accomplished style in old age. As Georges Wildenstein says, "It was not until circa 1760, that is aged sixty, that he reached his perfection."[10]

In his chosen genre of still life painting, Chardin was one of the great masters, and it was especially in this field that he excelled in his old age. Paintings such as *Still Life with Smoking Set* in the Louvre, painted between 1760 and 1763, the *Still Life with Wild Duck* in the Museum of Fine Arts in Springfield, Massachusetts, painted in 1764, and the *Peach Basket* of 1768, also in the Louvre, show him at his best and indicate that, far from deteriorating in old age, he actually improved on his earlier work. In his last years, apparently adversely affected by the smell of oil paint, Chardin had to give up painting, but this did not end his artistic career. He turned to pastel portraiture, achieving outstanding results in the field that had been considered the domain of Maurice Quentin de la Tour (1704–1788) and Rosalba Carriera (1675–1757), both of whom, incidentally, also lived into their eighties. Particularly fine are his self-portraits and his portrait of his wife. Chardin died at the age of eighty in the year 1779.

[10] Georges Wildenstein, *Chardin* (Zurich: Manesse, 1963), p. 11.

*Jean Baptiste Siméon Chardin*
Still Life with Wild Duck
*1764*
*Courtesy Museum of Fine Arts,*
*The James Philip Gray Collection,*
*Springfield, Massachusetts*

*Chardin Painted this work,* Still Life with Wild
Duck, *in 1764 at the age of sixty-five.*

Several of the Italian painters of this period also lived to an advanced age and continued working to the end of their lives. The earliest of these was Alessandro Magnasco, who was born in Genoa in 1667 and died there in 1749. He worked rapidly in a sketchy technique and his output was very large, much of it produced when he was an old man. After spending over two decades in Milan, he returned to his native city in 1735, when he was sixty-eight, and it was during these late years in Genoa that he painted some of his finest pictures. In these later canvases, his dramatic style, with its unnatural light and thick impasto, became ever more pronounced, and it is these works that are particularly admired by critics. Outstanding examples of such late paintings, which probably date from between 1735 and 1740, when he was around seventy, are the

*Alessandro Magnasco*
Landscape with Boat and Fisherman
*1735–1740*
*Courtesy The Metropolitan Museum of Art,*
*Punnett Fund, 1927, New York*

*Magnasco employed a sketchy painting technique in his* Landscape with Boat
and Fisherman, *thought to be painted between 1735 and 1740, the artist's
sixty-eighth and seventy-third years.*

*Synagogue* in The Cleveland Museum of Art, *The Garden Party* at
Albaro in the Palazzo Bianco in Genoa, and the *Landscape with
Boat and Fishermen* in The Metropolitan Museum of Art in New
York. Caterina Marcenaro gives a good description of his late style
in the *Encyclopedia of World Art*. It says, "Toward the end of his
life Magnasco's vision grew ever more fantastic, more evocative.
The images are ephemeral, phantasmagorical; bodily form, freed
from weight, exists only as color."[11]

[11] Caterina Marcenaro, in the *Encyclopedia of World Art*, vol. 9 (New York:
McGraw-Hill, 1964), p. 398.

A generation younger was the great Venetian master of the Rococo style, Giovanni Battista Tiepolo who was born in 1696. A much admired artist who enjoyed immense success not only in Venice but throughout Europe, he received numerous commissions in Venice and in many other Italian cities as well as abroad. He lived into old age and remained active to the end of his life. A typical work of his is the *Apollo Pursing Daphne* in The National Gallery in Washington, D.C. In 1755, when he was almost sixty and had just completed his celebrated paintings for the archbishop of Würzburg, he was elected president of the Venetian Art Academy, and six years later, at the age of sixty-five, he was invited by King Charles III to come to Madrid to decorate the Royal Palace. He arrived the following year

*Giovanni Battista Tiepolo*
Apollo Pursuing Daphne
*1755–1760*
*Courtesy National Gallery of Art,*
*Samuel H. Kress Collection, Washington, D.C.*

*The Venetian master Giovanni Battista Tiepolo painted* Apollo Pursuing Daphne *from 1755 to 1760, his fifty-ninth to sixty-fourth years.*

accompanied by his sons and assistants, and during the next four years, although nearing seventy, executed some of his biggest and most impressive paintings. The king next asked him to paint a large altarpiece, but he died while working on it in 1770, when he was seventy-four years old.

The third great Italian painter of the eighteenth century who lived very long and remained creative until late in life was the Venetian artist Francesco Guardi. He was much less famous than Tiepolo during his lifetime, but today is regarded as one of the greatest of all Venetian painters. Born in 1712 and dying at eighty-one in 1793, his life spans the century and his work is very characteristic of his age. His contemporaries saw him largely as a painter of picturesque views, a so-called Veduta painter, whose small pictures of Venice were intended for tourists who visited the famous Adriatic port city and wished to acquire souvenirs of their stay. In keeping with this, his output was vast and continued into his later years. Few of his works are dated but it is known that some of the most ambitious, such as the altarpiece at Roncegno in Valsugana and the depiction of the *Pope's Visit to Venice*, now in Oxford, date from the later years of his life, probably 1777 and 1782 respectively. A brilliant technician who used paint very freely and excelled in the portrayal of atmospheric effects, Guardi gave a vivid sense of the Venetian scene with the sunlight playing over the lagoons and buildings of his native city. His late work, with its very loose brushwork and brilliant use of color, was much admired by Turner and the Impressionists and in many ways anticipates their Venetian scenes.

In England there were several prominent artists of this period who reached old age and continued working into their later years. Outstanding among them was Henry Fuseli, who lived from 1741 to 1825. A native of Zurich, his real name was Johann Heinrich Füssli, but since he left his native Switzerland in 1763 when he was only twenty-three years old and spent the rest of his life in England, he is usually thought of as belonging to the English school. He was one of the most original painters of his age, especially in his late work,

*Francesco Guardi*
Campo San Zanipolo
*1782*
*Courtesy National Gallery of Art, Samuel H. Kress Collection, Washington, D.C.*

*Guardi's late works such as* Campo San Zanipolo, *painted in 1782 when the*
*artist was seventy, were greatly admired by Turner and the Impressionists.*

which shows an imaginative power that is quite extraordinary. Active to the very end of his life, he was appointed professor of painting at the Royal Academy when he was close to seventy and gave his famous lectures on art, which were published only after he died. At the time of his death at eighty-four, he was still at work on his last painting, which represents a scene from Shakespeare's *King John*. Fuseli was buried in St. Paul's Cathedral next to Sir Joshua Reynolds, who many years earlier had encouraged him to become a painter.

Among the many fine paintings of his late period, which started around 1800 when he was sixty, are his *Illustrations of Niebelungen Lied* and scenes from the writings of Shakespeare, Dante, and Homer as well as contemporary German and English poets. A true Romantic who was deeply steeped in the literature of German Romanticism, he did a series of pictures illustrating Friedrich de la Motte-Fouque's *Undine* that dates from the end of his life when he was eighty. One of his favorite themes, of which he painted many versions, was "The Nightmare" in which his imagination finds its most grotesque expression. A highly individualistic artist and a friend of William Blake's, Fuseli exemplified the unconventional artist of the Romantic movement at its most extravagant. This is also seen in his description of modern art, which according to him, ". . . is reared by superstition in Italy, taught to dance in France, plumped up to unwieldiness in Flanders, reduced to chronicle small

*J. H. Füssli (Fuseli)*
Murdered Woman and Furies
*1821*
*Courtesy Kunsthaus, Zurich*

*Fuseli was eighty when he painted* Murdered Woman and Furies *in 1821. It is one of his finest works.*

beer in Holland, became a rich old woman by suckling fools in England."[12]

A most interesting sculptor of this period who lived to be very old is Brazil's leading artist, Antonio Francisco Lisboa, who was born in 1730 of a Portuguese father, a prominent architect, and a black slave girl. A colorful and impulsive man, he showed considerable artistic talent when he was young, but it was not until his old age that his tremendous creativity and imaginative power manifested itself. When he was in his forties, he contracted a disease, probably leprosy, and became completely disfigured. He lost fingers and toes and became so repulsive that he shunned the public. Yet in spite of these handicaps, he continued working, fixing his pen or carving tools to the stump of his hand. So great was his desire to continue with his art and so remarkable was his determination that it was during these later years when he was crippled that he did some of his best work. His most famous carvings, the prophets at the Shrine of the Bom Jesus de Mateziuhos at Congonhes do Campo, were made between 1800 and 1805, between his seventieth and seventy-fifth years. He continued working to the very end of his life, signing his statutes in thin and even script. He died at the age of eighty-four in 1814.

If there was one art form that dominated the eighteenth century, it was architecture, and in this field several of the outstanding figures lived long lives and produced some of their finest work when they were past their sixtieth year. One of them was the great French architect Jacques Ange Gabriel, who was born in 1698 and lived to 1782, dying at the age of eighty-four. His first major work, the Galerie d'Ulysse at Fontainebleau, dates from 1737, but it was only in his maturity and old age that he was given the opportunity to develop his architectural ideas to their fullest under the rule of Louis XV, who had become a friend and patron of his. His masterpiece, exemplifying the classical Palladian ideals at their best, was the Petit

[12] R. Goldwater and M. Treves, *Artists on Art* (New York: Pantheon, 1945), p. 256.

J. A. Gabriel
Petit Trianon
1762–1768
Versailles

*Gabriel's masterpiece, the Petit Trianon, was under construction from 1762 to 1768, between the architect's sixty-fourth and seventieth years.*

Thomas Jefferson
Monticello
1820–1826
Charlottesville, Virginia

*Thomas Jefferson worked on his home, Monticello, almost to the day of his death at eighty-three in 1826.*

Trianon in the Gardens of Versailles, erected between 1762 and 1768, his sixty-fourth to seventieth years. The other outstanding work of his late period was his design for the Place Louis XV, today known as the Place de la Concorde, one of the most beautiful examples of urban planning and architectural design in all of Paris. It took a long period to complete this project, for it was started in 1735 and was not completed until twenty years later, when he was seventy years old.

In the United States the most remarkable architect of this period and one of the greatest men America has produced was Thomas Jefferson. He lived a very long life and it was especially during his later years, after he had retired from the presidency, that he devoted himself to architecture and designed his two most important projects. Born in 1743, he was already seventy-four when he started the University of Virginia and it was not completed until 1825, the year before his death. Commenting on the plan, he wrote to Judge Woodward, "Withdrawn by age from all the public services and attentions to public things I am closing the last scenes of my life by fashioning and fostering an establishment for the instruction of those who are to come after us. . . . The form and distribution of its structure are original and unique, the architecture chaste and classical, and the whole worthy of attracting the curiosity of a visit."[13] Although Jefferson was an old man at the time the project was conceived, this was, as he said, the most original and unique of his architectural designs and remains to this day the most beautiful university campus in the United States.

Several of the leading nineteenth-century painters who were particularly creative in their old age, such as Goya, Turner, Monet, and Cézanne, have already been discussed, but there were many others who continued to do fine work during their later years. Among the

[13] D. Guiness and J. T. Sadler, *Mr. Jefferson—Architect* (New York: Viking, 1973), p. 149.

Neoclassicists, Jacques Louis David and Jean Auguste Ingres are notable, with the former living to the age of seventy-seven and the latter reaching the age of eighty-seven. David, the older of the two, lived from 1748 to 1825 and was the leading artistic figure during the time of the French Revolution. However, after the Bourbon restoration of 1815, the artist, who at that time was sixty-seven, was forced to leave France and take refuge in Brussels, where he spent the rest of his life. Although his late work, in the eyes of most critics, does not live up to his earlier production, he continued painting until the time of his death a decade later. Works such as *Mars Disarmed by Venus* in the Royal Art Museum in Brussels exemplify this late style. While still showing his considerable skill and his characteristic manner, they would nevertheless suggest that, as Walter Friedlaender said, "He lacked those large inner ideas, with which such geniuses as Titian, Rembrandt and Poussin overcame the natural physical decline and rose to the sublime."[14]

While this judgment no doubt applies to his mythological scenes such as the *Cupid and Psyche* of 1817 in the Collection Murat in Paris or *Leonides at Thermopylae* of 1814, now in the Louvre, which David himself considered one of the masterpieces in which he had realized the Greek ideal, it is not a fair assessment of the portraits of his old age, for in this field his remarkable gifts are still clearly visible. In these canvases, based on nature rather than myth and painted in a more realistic style, the aged artist is still seen at his very best. Works such as the *Three Ladies of Ghent* of 1818, now in the Louvre, his *M. Greindl* of 1816, and the lovely *Nude Study*, which is believed to have been painted around 1824, a year before his death, show the artist, now in his seventies, in full command of his powers.

Even more remarkable was Ingres, who lived ten years longer than David, for he was born in 1780 and died in 1867, and painted some of his greatest works when he was already an elderly man. In fact, his alertness and his desire for further growth were so great that

[14] Walter Friedlaender, *David to Delacroix* (Cambridge, Mass.: Harvard University Press, 1952), p. 32.

*David painted* Cupid and Psyche, *a mythological scene, in 1817 while in exile from France. He was sixty-nine.*

when he was in his eighties, he went to a connoisseur's house in order to copy a portrait of Mary Tudor attributed to Holbein. When asked why he wished to do so, he replied, "To learn." At eighty-six, close to his death, he made a drawing after Giotto. In 1855, when he was seventy-five, the largest exhibit of his work was held at the Exposition Universalle. Two years previously he was commissioned to paint a large picture representing the *Apotheosis of Napoleon I*, which the emperor Napoleon III and his empress personally inspected in his studio. And when he painted his self-portrait at the age of eighty-five, he depicted himself as a handsome, well-preserved, self-assured man, confident that he was still in full control of his great gifts.

Among the many splendid works of his old age are pictures such as the portrait of the *Comtesse d'Haussonville of 1845*, now in

*J. A. D. Ingres*
Comtesse d'Haussonville
*1845*
*Copyright The Frick Collection, New York*

*Ingres was sixty-five when he painted the splendid portrait of the Comtesse*
*d'Haussonville in 1845.*

the Frick Collection in New York, the picture of Mme Moitessier of
1856 now in the National Gallery in London, and the superb painting of the Princesse de Broglie of 1858 in the collection of the
Duchess de Broglie in Paris. Interestingly enough, some of Ingres's

finest nudes were also painted during the late years of his life, notably the *Turkish Women at the Bath* in the Louvre, a sensuous evocation of a harem that was painted in 1862 when he was a man in his eighties. While his late works of religious or mythological scenes may not appeal as much to the modern taste, pictures such as *Christ Among the Doctors*, his last painting, which was still in his studio at the time of his death, were greatly admired by his contemporaries. He died a man of eighty-seven, confident of his place in the history of French painting, and left some of his pictures, his notebooks, and his library to the Ingres Museum in his native town of Montauban.

The transition from Classicism to Romanticism is well exemplified by the English painter William Blake, who did some of his finest work during the last years of his life, when he was between sixty and seventy years of age. Born in 1757, he died in 1827 at which time, after long years of struggle and poverty, he was enjoying a certain amount of success and was much admired by a group of young artists who called themselves the Ancients and numbered among their members such well-known figures as Fuseli, Palmer, and Calvert. His patron during the years was his friend John Linnel, who

*William Blake*
When the Morning Stars Sang Together
*1826*
*Courtesy Museum of Fine Arts,*
*Gift of Miss Ellen Bullard,*
*Boston*

*Blake engraved this illustration for*
The Book of Job *in 1826, the year*
*before his death at seventy.*

125

commissioned his two last great works, the illustrations for the Book of Job, consisting of twenty-one large watercolors produced during the early 1820s and engraved in 1826, and the one hundred two illustrations of Dante's *Divine Comedy* made between 1824 and 1827, the year of his death. These works show Blake's highly individual and visionary style at its peak and have often been described as his most satisfying artistic expression.

A French artist who lived a very long life and changed from the formal classical style of his youth to a more lyrical, romantic one in his old age was Jean Baptiste Camille Corot, who lived from 1796 to 1875. A vigorous artist who remained in excellent health almost to the end of his life, he was described when he visited the 1874 Salon as "... still an impressive figure, showing few signs of the infirmities of old age."[15] In the summer of that year he painted one of his finest pictures, the *Interior of Sens Cathedral*, now in the Louvre. Although he became ill with cancer in the fall of 1874, he continued to paint and submitted three large pictures to the Salon of 1875, but before the exhibition opened, he had died, much lamented by all. His last paintings, such as the *Girl from Albano* of 1872, now in The Brooklyn Museum, *Mademoiselle de Fondras*, also of 1872 and now in Glasgow, *The Gypsy Girl with a Mandolin* of 1874 in the Sao Paolo Museum in Brazil, and the full-length *Lady in Blue* of 1874 in the Louvre, are placed among his masterpieces and show that he remained creative to the very end of his long life.

In addition to Monet, who reached the age of eighty-six, two other French Impressionists lived to be old: Renoir, who died at seventy-eight, and Degas who lived to eighty-three. Although both suffered from infirmities in their old age, this did not stop them from working into their last years. Renoir, who was born in 1841, a year after Monet, died in 1919, a crippled old man who had been confined to a wheelchair since 1912 and had seen his two sons badly wounded in the battles of the First World War. In fact, since 1898, when he was

[15] J. Leymarie, *Corot*, translated by S. Gilbert (Lausanne: Skira, 1966), p. 107.

*Jean Baptiste Camille Corot*
Gypsy Girl with a Mandolin
*1870–1875*
*Courtesy National Gallery of Art,*
*Gift of Count Cecil Pecci-Blunt,*
*1951,*
*Washington, D.C.*

Corot's Gypsy Girl with a
Mandolin *was painted during*
*the last five years of the artist's*
*life. He died in 1875 at the age*
*of seventy-nine.*

fifty-seven years old, he had suffered from arthritis that had grown
steadily worse until he was forced to strap his brush to his wrist and
to depend upon his wife's help when he wished to wipe away some
paint. Yet despite this, such was his vitality that during the last years
of his life he developed a completely new style, which went beyond
Impressionism. As Parker Tyler says, "The disease did not let up
during the nineties and the new century that progressively crippled
the great painter, who went forward nevertheless with grander and
grander nudes."[16]

Employing a more monumental and plastic style, Renoir in his
old age broke with the Impressionistic tenets of his earlier period.
Using ever simpler forms and emphasizing mass and color at the
expense of line, these late works sing hymns of praise to the sensuous beauty of the female body. Like Rubens and Watteau before
him, the aged Renoir celebrated the nude at the very time when a
younger generation of painters was embracing the Cubist aesthetics

[16] Parker Tyler, *Renoir* (New York: Doubleday, 1968), p. 100.

*Pierre Auguste Renoir*
Tilla Durieux
*1914*
*Courtesy The Metropolitan*
*Museum of Art,*
*Bequest of Stephen C. Clark, 1960,*
*New York*

*Renoir at the advanced age of*
*seventy-three continued to revel in*
*the female form, as can be seen in*
*his 1914 portrait of Tilla Durieux.*

in which the female figure was reduced to an abstract, geometric design. For Renoir, at this time in his seventies, it was the fullness of the body form, the light reflected on the flesh, and the beauty of color that remained all important, as is evident in such masterpieces, now in the Louvre, as *The Reclining Nude, Back View* of 1909, *Gabrielle with a Rose* of 1911, and the *Grande Nude* of 1912 and the *Tilla Durieux* in The Metropolitan Museum in New York.

Degas, who lived from 1834 to 1917, lived to be even older than Renoir, dying when he was well into his eighties. Like Daumier, he was troubled by poor eyesight in his old age, a condition that entered a critical phase in 1892 when he was fifty-eight years old. First he had to give up oil painting and then about 1904 to 1906, he became almost completely blind. But this did not stop him from working, in spite of his bitter remark that "Everything is trying for a blind man who wants to make believe that he can see."[17] Prevented

17 Edouard Huettinger, *Degas* (New York: Crown, 1977), p. 84.

from painting in oil, he turned increasingly to pastels and sculptures of ballerinas and horses, which today are considered among his greatest artistic achievements. However, at the very end of his life, now almost completely sightless, he was unable to work, and it is said that he wandered through the streets of Paris like a blind Homer, no longer able to see the world around him.

Degas's last public exhibition was held in 1893, when he was only fifty-nine years old, but this did not mean that he had given up working, for his devotion to art had in no way diminished despite his infirmity. Pastels, pencil sketches, and charcoal drawings, gouaches, monotypes, and works in mixed media, such as his superb little landscapes of 1889 to 1892, continued to occupy him, and it is among these works that some of his most sensitive and aesthetically rewarding pictures are to be found. Pastels, such as *After the Bath* of 1898, produced when he was sixty-four, and the *Bath* of 1890 in the Art Institute of Chicago, are certainly among his true master-pieces, and the bronzes of these late years are not only the finest sculptures made by any painter of the time but, next to those of Rodin, the best works in this medium of this period. A lonely recluse whose friends and contemporaries had predeceased him, Degas died

*Edgar Degas*
Developpé en Avant
*c. 1915*
*Courtesy The Metropolitan Museum of Art,*
*Bequest of Mrs. H. O. Havemeyer, 1929,*
*H. O. Havemeyer Collection, New York*

*It is believed that this statuette,* Developpé en Avant, *was made when the artist was in his seventies; it was not cast until his death in 1917.*

at eighty-three on September 27, 1917, an event little noticed, since everyone's attention was focused on the Great War.

Both the outstanding American painters of the nineteenth century, Winslow Homer and Thomas Eakins, lived into their seventies and produced some of their finest work in their old age. Homer, who lived from 1836 to 1910, was a true New Englander. Born in Boston, he spent most of his mature life in Prouts Neck, Maine, where he had built himself a house and studio directly on the sea. From there he could observe and paint the ocean in all its moods and appearances, a theme he never tired of. Typical of this kind of painting for which he became famous are the *Northeaster* in The Metropolitan Museum of Art, which was painted in 1895 when he was fifty-nine years old, *The Lookout—"All's Well"* of the following year in the Museum of Fine Arts in Boston, *Early Morning after a Storm at Sea* of 1902 in The Cleveland Museum of Art, all painted in his old age. They are realistic and vivid depictions of the seascape as he observed it outdoors off the rocky coast of Maine, for as he once said, "I wouldn't go across the street to see a Bougereau. His pictures look false . . . his light is not outdoor light; his works are waxy and artificial."[18]

While he spent most of the year in Maine, during the winter he often made trips to the Bahamas, Cuba, Florida, and Bermuda, where he painted watercolors that many critics consider among his best works. Those of 1898 and 1899, when he was in his middle sixties, have a special freshness and spontaneity never found in his oils, and these pictures inspired countless later American watercolor painters. As Lloyd Goodrich said, "His handling had never been freer, his brush drawing surer, combining softness and absolute mastery. . . . In watercolor his temperament found its perfect medium."[19] Pictures such as the *Rum Cay* of 1898 in the Worcester Art Museum, the *Turtle Pond*, also of 1898, in The Brooklyn Museum, and *Palm Tree, Nassau* of 1898 in The Metropolitan Museum of Art are indeed the high points of his career.

[18] Goldwater and Treves, *Artists*, p. 353.
[19] Lloyd Goodrich, *Winslow Homer* (New York: Macmillan, 1945), p. 159.

*Winslow Homer*
Palm Tree, Nassau
*1898*
*Courtesy The Metropolitan*
*Museum of Art,*
*Purchase, Amelia B. Lazarus*
*Fund, 1910,*
*New York*

Palm Tree, Nassau *was one of*
*many outstanding watercolors*
*Winslow Homer executed in*
*1898, when he was sixty-two.*

The other great American painter of the period was Thomas Eakins, who was a decade younger than Homer, for he was born in 1844 and died, aged seventy-two, in 1916. A native Philadelphian, he spent most of his life there with the exception of a few years in Paris, where he studied with Gerome, and a visit to Spain where he was much impressed with the work of Velázquez. A painter, sculptor, photographer, and teacher who introduced drawing from the nude into the curriculum of the Pennsylvania Academy of Art, where he taught for many years, Eakins was an artist of great versatility, although it was in portraiture that he particularly excelled. While he had also painted genre scenes earlier in life, during his old age he concentrated almost entirely on portraits, which are among the greatest paintings of their kind in the history of American art. These pictures were a true labor of love and Eakins often selected the persons to be painted and presented them with the finished pictures.

They were uncompromising in their realism and, especially in his last years, profound in their interpretation of character. Paintings such as *Professor Leslie Miller* of 1901 in the Philadelphia Museum and the portrait *Mrs. Edith Mahon* of 1904, painted when he was sixty, now in the Smith College Museum, exemplify Eakins at his best and are among the masterpieces of American art.

By far the greatest sculptor of the nineteenth century in Europe was Auguste Rodin, who lived from 1840 to 1917 and continued working almost to the end of his life. However, it is generally agreed that all his best work was done before his sixtieth birthday and that the carvings of his last years were minor in scale and often executed largely by his assistants. The last of his truly great works was the statue of Balzac of 1898, which was finished when he was fifty-eight years old. The climax of his career occurred in 1900 when, during the World Exposition of that year, a large show of Rodin's work was placed on display in a specially built pavilion and his *Thinker* was bought by public subscription and presented to the people of Paris, who placed it in front of the Pantheon in 1906. After this, Rodin became the most celebrated sculptor of modern times. His studio was visited by every person of importance who came to Paris, young artists such as Meunier vied with each other to work in his atelier, and distinguished writers such as Rainer Maria Rilke became his secretaries. His fame and influence spread throughout Europe and even reached Japan, where he had a whole school of devoted admirers and imitators.

Despite this adulation, or perhaps because of it, his artistic output of the last two decades was not up to his earlier work. He continued to receive numerous commissions and he made portrait busts of many well-known people, among them George Bernard Shaw, Joseph Pulitzer, Gustav Mahler, and Georges Clemenceau as well as the Pope Benedict XV. The last of these busts, on which he was still working at the time of his death in 1917, was that of the minister of commerce, Etienne Clemental. The most personal and most expressive of these is the head of the Japanese dancer Hanoko, of which he made several versions. However, the most interesting works of his old age are the various female figures such as the *Torso of a Young Woman* of 1909, the *Half-length Figure of a Woman* of 1910 and the *Dance Movement D* of 1911, all three now in the Delbanco Collection in Larchmont, New York. These fragmentary figures rendered in a rather abstract style have a vitality and expressive power that the rather conventional portrait busts lack and show that the elderly master was still capable at times of great artistic achievements.

Several of the leading architects of the nineteenth century also lived long lives and did some of their most important work during their later years. In England it was above all John Nash, who was born in 1752 and died in 1835, who executed some of his most remarkable projects during his old age. Outstanding among these was his grandiose scheme for the creation of the Royal Mile, extending from Regent's Park with its terraces through Park Crescent and Regent Street to Carlton House, an ambitious plan that occupied him from 1811 to 1827, from his sixtieth to his seventy-fifth years. Although his design was never carried out in its entirety and the colonnade in Regent Street was demolished in 1848, the part which still exists, notably Regent's Park, Regent Street, Park Crest, and the Chester and Cumberland terraces with their excellent layout and harmonious Neoclassical proportions, are among the finest examples of urban planning and architectural design in all of London.

The other notable example of Nash's late style is the Brighton Pavilion of 1815 to 1821, built for the Prince of Wales, later George IV, who was his greatest patron. The structure had originally been erected in an Indian Mogul style by Repton, but it was extended and transformed by Nash with Gothic and Chinese detail and frank use of structural cast iron. A highly original and excellently carried out piece of architectural design, it shows Nash, who was almost seventy when the building was completed, at the height of his power. The other great architectural enterprise of his old age was the re-designing of Buckingham Palace, a commission he also received from the Prince of Wales. He was engaged in this important project between 1826 and 1830, when he was a man in his middle and late seventies, but the death of his patron and the change in artistic taste put an end to his work on this scheme, which was completed by

*John Nash*
*Royal Pavilion*
*1815–1821*
*Brighton, England*

*A notable example of Nash's innovative style is the Royal Pavilion at Brighton. Nash was almost seventy when the structure was completed.*

other architects in a style very different from that which Nash had planned. He died a few years later, in 1835, at the age of eighty-three.

In the United States, one of the most interesting architects of this period who did some of his best work in his late years was Frederick Law Olmsted, who was born in 1822 and died in 1903. Primarily a landscape architect, his major work is Central Park in New York City, which he designed when he was still a young man with his partner Calvert Vaux. The first and most important American working in this field, he defined the function of a park in these words: "The purpose is to provide opportunity for a form of recreation to be obtained only through the influence of pleasing natural scenery upon the sensibilities of those quietly contemplating it. The larger part of the property, being the division designated 'The Country Part' is proposed to be set apart with absolute exclusiveness of purpose. That is to say, if this part of the park is to have value for any other purpose, it is designated that it shall occur incidentally, and at no appreciable sacrifice of advantages for the quiet enjoyment of natural scenery."[20]

Continuing his remarkable career as a pioneer in landscape architecture, Olmsted received commissions from all over the country, many of them when he was in his sixties and early seventies. In 1885, at the age of sixty-three, he was called to Boston to design the Franklin Park. Between 1874 and 1895 he worked in the District of Columbia and in 1890, when he was in his late sixties, he was called to Chicago to plan the layout of the grounds for the 1893 World's Fair Columbian Exhibition. This great project and the design for Biltmore, the Vanderbilt estate in North Carolina, on which he was engaged between 1893 and 1895, his sixty-ninth to his seventy-third years, were the crowning achievements of his career. In 1895 he was forced to give up his professional practice, since his mind was failing, and he spent the remainder of his life in the McLean Asylum in Waverly, Massachusetts. He died in 1903 at the age of eighty-one.

[20] J. Fabos, C. Milde and M. Weinmayr, *Frederick Law Olmsted Sr.* (Amherst, Mass.: University of Massachusetts Press, 1968), p. 68.

In the Far East there were many artists who reached old age and produced some of their best work during the later years of their life. While there are no records relating to the lives of the architects and sculptors, since they were considered mere artisans, there are many accounts of the careers of famous painters and calligraphers, and their scrolls often have inscriptions indicating when they were made. The earliest of these painters whose old-age work can be documented is Huang Kung-wang, an artist of the Yuan period, who lived from 1269 to 1354. Not only did he live to the ripe old age of eighty-five, but we are told that he ended his life as a Taoist hermit living close to nature in the Fu-ch'an Mountains, which inspired some of his best-known scrolls. His most celebrated painting, which is considered one of the great masterpieces of Chinese art and has inspired innumerable other pictures, is a long scroll now in the National Palace Museum in Taipei. Dated 1347, it was done during his seventy-eighth year. A magnificent mountain landscape executed in the sparse, restrained style characteristic of the Yuan period and painted with a very dry brush, it shows the master at his best, indicating that far from declining in his old age, he was reaching the height of his artistic creativity. This is not too surprising, for in traditional China, in keeping with Confucian teaching, old age was venerated so that it was widely believed that only when an artist had reached his advanced years, experienced life to the full, and rid himself of the passions and tensions of youth could he attain the kind of detached wisdom that would enable him to give expression to the innermost secrets of nature or, as the Chinese would have said, to the eternal tao that penetrates all being.

The greatest Japanese painter of his period was Sesshu, who lived from 1420 to 1506. A Zen monk and ink painter, he is regarded by many critics as the foremost of all Japanese artists. In middle age he traveled to China to visit Buddhist temples and study the art there, and it was after his return to Japan that he reached his artistic maturity and became the leading painter of his day. His greatest masterpieces are his large landscape scroll of 1486, painted when he

*Sesshu*
Landscape in the Cursive Style
Haboku Sansui
*1496*
*Courtesy Collection of National
Museum,
Tokyo*

*Sesshu's* Landscape in the
Cursive Style *of 1496, painted in
his seventy-sixth year, is a
characteristic work of the
Japanese master's old age.*

was sixty-six years old, which is the Zen picture of the Priest Hui-ko
cutting off his arm, and above all the magnificent *Hoboku Sansui* of
1496 in the Tokyo National Museum, painted when he was seventy-
six, and usually considered the most inspired of all Japanese landscape paintings.

Although none of the sixteenth-century painters equal these masters
in their greatness or influence, several were outstanding artists and
lived to an advanced age. In China there were Wen Cheng-ming,
who was born in 1470 and died at eighty-nine in 1559, and Tung
Ch'i-ch'ang, who lived from 1555 to 1636, dying in his eighty-first
year. Both these artists were the very essence of the Chinese literati,
men who devoted their lives to scholarship, poetry, calligraphy, and
especially painting and were much admired by their contemporaries
and by later generations of artists and scholars. Both not only remained active in their late years but also painted some of their
greatest scrolls when they were elderly men. Of Wen Cheng-ming it

*Wen Cheng-ming*
The Seven Thuja Trees
*1532*
*Courtesy Honolulu Academy of Arts, Gift of Mrs. Carter Galt, 1952*

*The Seven Thuja Trees of 1532 is one of Wen Cheng-ming's most famous works. It was painted in the artist's sixty-second year.*

was said, "Though he grew very old, reaching over eighty, the brightness of his spirit did not fade. He used to sketch with ink and paper even by lamplight, and therefore, the collectors treasured his works like pieces of ceremonial jade."[21] Outstanding among his surviving works are the *Juniper* scroll of 1532 in the Honolulu Academy of Arts and the painting of the same subject in the Nelson Gallery in Kansas City, which is believed to have been painted in 1550 when the artist was already eighty.

In seventeenth-century China artists of the academic school and the so-called Eccentric school lived very long and immensely creative lives. Typical of the former were Wang Shih-min, who reached the age of eighty-eight, for he was born in 1592 and died in 1680, and Wang Hui, who was a generation younger, living from 1632 to 1717. A contemporary critic commenting on the old-age work of the former had this to say: "It is certainly the best work done by the painter. He was very old when he painted it, yet still full of vigor, bright and alert, not inferior to a young man."[22] In fact there can be no doubt that his artistic creativity reached its climax in his old age after he retired from his duties as a government official.

[21] Osvald Siren, *Chinese Painting*, vol. 4 (New York: Ronald Press, 1958), p. 173.
[22] Ibid., p. 101.

Judging from the inscriptions on his paintings, the year 1688, when he was almost seventy-five, was his best time in regard to both the quality and the quantity of his production. In 1670, when he was close to eighty, an inscription on a picture of *Wooded Mountains Rising Through Mist* complains of approaching old age and weakness of his wrist, but six years later in 1676, when he was eighty-four, he was still capable of producing a very fine flower painting.

His pupil Wang Hui also lived to be very old and continued to be creative to the end of his long life. His output must have been vast, for many of his scrolls survive to this day, with outstanding pictures by his hand found in the National Palace Museum in Taipei and in the collection of Mr. Earl Morse of New York City, who has specialized in the work of this artist. Among these pictures

*Wang Hui*
The Wisteria Studio
*1712*
*Courtesy The Art Museum, Princeton University,*
*Gift of Mr. and Mrs. Earl Morse,*
*Princeton, New Jersey*

The Wisteria Studio *by Wang Hui was painted in 1712, the master's eightieth year.*

are two that come from the very last years of his life and show him at the top of his form, the *Landscape in the Style of Ni Tsan* of 1710 and the *Wisteria Studio in the Style of Wang Meng* of 1712, his eightieth year. An even later painting with the date of 1717, the year of his death, is the picture of *Leafless Trees and Blackbirds by a Stream*, formerly in the Yamamoto collection.

The two most original and interesting Chinese painters of the early Ch'ing period were Chu Ta and Tao-chi. They were close friends and belonged to the Eccentric school of Chinese painting that is particularly admired by modern artists and collectors. Both of them lived to be old men, for Chu Ta lived from 1626 to 1705, which by Chinese reckoning made him eighty at the time of his death, while Tao-chi was about seventy-eight, having been born in 1641 and dying about 1720. The former was a tremendously creative artist who produced a huge body of work during his long life. However, since few of these paintings are dated, it is difficult to be certain about their chronology. Their subjects are mostly birds, flowers, and fish painted in a very forceful, abstract style that has much in common with modern art. That some of these pictures must date from his old age is indicated by a letter from Tao-chi in which his friend says, "You, master, have now reached the age of seventy-four, but you still climb mountains as if endowed with wings, you are truly

*Chu Ta*
Birds and Lotus Pond
*1690*
*Courtesy the Cincinnati Art Museum*

*The scrolls representing* Birds and Lotus Pond *of 1690 illustrate the power of Chu Ta's art as he entered his sixty-fourth year.*

*Tao-chi*
The Peach Blossom Spring
*c. 1710*
*Courtesy Freer Gallery of Art Library,*
*Smithsonian Institution, Washington, D.C.*

*It is believed that Tao-chi painted this hand scroll, entitled* The Peach Blossom
Spring, *late in his life. He died at seventy-six.*

one of the Immortals."[23] That this is indeed true is illustrated by the
scroll *Birds and Lotus Pond*, dated 1690, and now in the Cincinnati
Art Museum.

Tao-chi's old-age style can be seen in the *Mountain Landscape
in the Manner of Ni Tsan* of 1701 in the collection of Mr. C. C.
Wang of New York and in the album of 1703 in Boston's Museum
of Fine Arts, both of which show him at the very height of his
power. Even later, dating from a time when he was in his middle
sixties, is his *Peach Blossom Spring* in the collection of the Freer
Gallery in Washington, D.C. A highly original and very individual
artist, Tao-chi, who also called himself Shih-t'ao, was one of the
most varied and fascinating of all Chinese painters. He especially
excelled in landscapes and flower pieces rendered in an inspired,
very unorthodox style, which he maintained into his old age.

[23] Ibid., p. 156.

In Japan, several outstanding artists of the Edo period, which lasted from 1615 to 1868, led very long and creative lives. Most interesting is probably the leading Zen painter, Hakuin, who lived from 1685 to 1768, reaching the age of eighty-three. He was a very prolific artist and a large number of works attributed to him have survived. However, the dating and even the authenticity of many of these works remain in doubt. It is estimated that there are some eight thousand scrolls attributed to Hakuin, many of them no doubt spurious. It is generally agreed that some of the best were painted in his old age when his clerical duties no longer occupied so much of

*Hakuin*
Monkey Reaching for Reflection of Moon
*Edo Period, Eighteenth Century*
*Collection Hugo Munsterberg,*
*New Paltz, New York*

*The Zen master Hakuin painted* Monkey Reaching for Reflection of Moon, *along with many other of his best works, during his last years. He was eighty-three years old when he died in 1768.*

his time, for he had spent most of his life as an abbot of a Zen temple and a teacher of Buddhism. While many of his pictures are specifically Buddhist in character, such as the *Monkey Reaching for Reflection of Moon*, others are portraits, landscapes, animals, and flowers, all of which are painted in a very free, inspired style.

In the twentieth century, there are numerous artists who lived into old age and were very active during their late years, and as life expectancy increases, the number of such persons will no doubt grow ever larger. Some of the most remarkable, such as Matisse, Bonnard, Nevelson, and Kahn, have already been discussed in earlier chapters, while others, such as Picasso, de Chirico, and Chagall will be treated later. However, this still leaves such a large number that only those who seem to be the most significant and who continued to produce on a very high level can be discussed.

Among American architects, the one who exemplifies this best is Frank Lloyd Wright, who not only lived to be a very old man but was also engaged in the completion of his last great masterpiece, The Solomon R. Guggenheim Museum in New York, at the time of his death at ninety-two in 1959. Born in 1867 in Wisconsin, he had already made very important contributions to modern architecture, but it was in his late years that some of his finest designs were produced. He remained youthful and spry even when he was an old man. Peter Blake says, "As he grew older, he seemed to grow more beautiful also: his flowing silver hair, his erect figure, looking much taller than he really was, his weathered and bronze face—he put on quite a show . . . Wright seemed never to grow old. When he celebrated his eightieth birthday, he talked about moving farther out into the Arizona deserts in ten years or twenty because the lights and telegraph lines of civilization were beginning to intrude upon the views from Taliesin West."[24]

The work of Wright's later years that shows the full development of his artistic style starts with the Kaufmann House at Bear

24 Peter Blake, *Master Builders* (New York: Norton, 1960), p. 368.

ABOVE:
*Frank Lloyd Wright*
*Solomon R. Guggenheim Museum,*
*1950–1959*
*Photo Courtesy Solomon R.*
*Guggenheim Museum,*
*New York*

LEFT:
*Frank Lloyd Wright*
*Solomon R. Guggenheim Museum,*
*Interior*
*1950–1959*
*Photo Courtesy Solomon R.*
*Guggenheim Museum,*
*New York*

*Frank Lloyd Wright worked on his last commission, the Guggenheim Museum, from 1950 to the time of his death in 1959 at a remarkable ninety-two years of age.*

Run, Pennsylvania, which was completed in 1937, when he was seventy years old, and the Johnson Wax Company factory in Racine, Wisconsin, erected between 1936 and 1939. These are two of his most famous and original designs. After this, Wright, who in his earlier life often had difficulty getting commissions, was inundated with requests for buildings not only from the United States but from all over the world. The last two decades of his life, when he was between seventy and ninety, were his busiest and saw the execution of some of his finest designs, such as the campus for Florida Southern College at Lakeland, built between 1940 and 1950; his own winter home at Taliesin West near Phoenix, Arizona, begun in 1938 and continuing to the time of his death; the Laboratory Tower of the Johnson Wax Company factory in 1950; and The Solomon R. Guggenheim Museum on Fifth Avenue in New York, which occupied him during the last decade of his life.

Even these masterpieces were only a small part of his output. With the youthful enthusiasm and creative energy of a man half his age, Wright poured out a wealth of different designs, varying all the way from inexpensive homes for ordinary people to purely fantastic projects such as the Mile High Tower, his scheme for the Golden Triangle area in downtown Pittsburgh, and his opera house for Baghdad. He was also a prolific writer, a brilliant speaker, and a public figure who enjoyed airing his often unpopular and, in the realm of politics, sometimes offensive views. His position during his old age was one not occupied by any other American artist before or since, for he was a man of towering genius, the greatest architect this country has produced and, in the eyes of some, the greatest architect of all times. When he died shortly before his ninety-second birthday, it could truly be said that a giant had passed from the American scene.

Another of the great masters of modern architecture who lived a long and productive life was the Swiss-born French architect Le Corbusier, pseudonym of Charles Edouard Jeanneret. Born in 1887, he died in 1965 at the age of seventy-eight and continued to work to the end of his life. Like Wright, he had already made a significant contribution to twentieth-century architecture as a young man, both in terms of actual buildings and even more in his theories; but it was only during the post–World War Two period, when he was in his sixties, that he had the opportunity to erect a large number of buildings. Peter Blake, speaking of Le Corbusier in his old age, puts it this way:

> Corbu had done his bit—and much more—for modern architecture and might well be permitted to rest on his laurels. He did nothing of the sort: at St. Die and at Marseilles he created two concepts of such staggering boldness and beauty that most of his devoted followers in other parts of the world were left far behind, still playing around with the forms of a Ville Contemporaine or a Swiss Pavilion of the 20's and 30's. Corbu far from settling down to the peaceful role of Elder Statesman, had opened up several new vistas. Fifteen years later the younger architects of Europe, Asia and the Americas were only just beginning to grasp the lessons of St. Die and Marseilles.[25]

Beginning with the great apartment house complex called Unité d'habitation, designed to house some sixteen hundred people under one roof along with all kinds of facilities and a shopping center, which was erected between 1947 and 1952, Le Corbusier emerged as the most original and influential of modern architects. Equally impressive was his design for the pilgrimage church of Notre Dame de Ronchamps of 1950 to 1955 with its massive concrete forms and strange space, more like a huge piece of sculpture than a traditional building, which broke completely with the functional ideas of the Bauhaus.

Now a man close to seventy, Le Corbusier became the most sought-after architect in the world, with followers in Europe, America, and especially Japan, where several leading architects had been his students. In 1957 he was called to Berlin to design an apartment for a newly rebuilt section of the city. Harvard invited him to build the Carpenter Center in Cambridge, Massachusetts, and Japan asked him to come to Tokyo to build a structure for its new Art Museum. He was called to Ahmedabad to design a building there,

[25] Ibid., p. 113.

*Le Corbusier*
*Notre-Dame-du-Haut*
*1950–1955*
*Ronchamp, France*

*Le Corbusier's impressive sculptural church, Notre-Dame-du-Haut in*
*Ronchamp, France, was begun in 1950 and completed five years later when the*
*architect was sixty-eight.*

and in France he was commissioned to build a Dominican novitiate
monastery at Ste. Marie de la Tourette at Eveux near Lyons, which
was to be one of his most interesting and influential structures.
However, the most ambitious project of his old age was the plan for
a new capital for the East Punjab at Chandigarh where, in the foot-
hills of the Himalayas, he proposed to create a complete urban center that would eventually house some half million people. Assisted
by his brother Pierre Jeanneret, the English architects Jane Drew
and Maxwell Fry, and a staff of Indian architects and engineers, he
created his masterpieces, which represent the culmination of everything he had worked for and advocated during his life. In discussing
Chandigarh, H. H. Arnason says, "Le Corbusier's achievement is
embodied not only in one individual building, but in their subtle
visual relationship to one another. The total complex, to be completed by another building designed as a Governor's residence or
Museum, constitutes a fitting climax to Corbusier's career."[26] Out-

26 H. Horvard Arnason, *History of Modern Art* (New York: Prentice-Hall, 1968),
p. 442.

standing among these structures are the Secretariat of 1952–1956, and above all, the magnificent High Court of Justice, which was completed in 1956, on the eve of his seventieth birthday. Yet he continued working for almost an entire decade until his death in 1965.

The third of the great masters of modern architecture who reached an advanced age and remained active to the time of his death was the German-born American architect Ludwig Mies van der Rohe. Born in 1886, a year before Le Corbusier, he outlived him by four years, dying in 1969 at the age of eighty-three. He too had done very important work as a younger man in his native Germany, but it was not until he came to the United States after the rise of Hitler that he was able to realize his architectural ideas on a large scale. As the head of the architectural school of the Illinois Institute of Technology in Chicago, he was given the task of designing a new campus for this school, a project that occupied him from 1940 to 1943. A man of the twentieth century, he was trying to reflect our age in his designs. As he said, "I didn't want to change the time. I wanted to express the time. That was my whole object. I didn't want to change anything. I really believe that all these ideas, the sociological ideas and even the technological ideas, would have an influence on architecture. But they are not architecture themselves. What we really need is to know how to build with any material, and that is what is missing today."[27]

In 1947, to celebrate the artist's sixtieth birthday, The Museum of Modern Art in New York staged a large retrospective, which proved a great success and established him as one of the leading architects in the United States. But no one could have foreseen the long years of artistic creativity that were still ahead of him. Structures of all types, from tall apartment houses like those erected in 1951 on Lake Shore Drive in Chicago, to beautiful private homes such as the Farnsworth House in Fox River, Illinois, built between 1946 and 1950, established him as the leader in the International

[27] Peter Blake, "A Conversation with Mies, Record of Symposium at the School of Architecture," Columbia, May 1961, New York, 1963, p. 104.

*Mies van der Rohe*
*Seagram Building*
*1958*
*New York*

*The crowning masterpiece of*
*Mies van der Rohe's career was*
*the Seagram Building in New*
*York, which opened in 1958*
*when the architect was*
*seventy-two.*

school of modern architecture. Perhaps his most impressive and well-known structure is the Seagram Building, which was opened in 1958 when he was seventy-two years old. A thirty-eight-story bronze-and-glass tower located on Park Avenue in New York City, it is probably the most accomplished and elegant of all the great skyscrapers of the postwar period. With its beautiful open space in front and its steeply rising vertical forms, it represents modern architecture at its very best and combines excellence of design with the beautiful use of building materials.

At this stage of his life, a man in his seventies, Mies van der Rohe had reached the pinnacle of his career. Commissions were coming in from all over the world and his influence was felt everywhere. In 1963 he was asked to plan a Federal Center for downtown Chicago and to design a new National Gallery for his native country in Berlin, which he completed in 1968 shortly before his death. The State Department requested a design for a new American consulate general in Sao Paolo, Brazil, in 1959, and the Bacardi Company asked him to plan new headquarters in Mexico City in 1961. In 1959 Queen Elizabeth awarded him the Royal Gold Medal for Architecture; in 1960 the American Institute of Architects gave him their Gold Medal for outstanding achievement; and he also received honors and medals in his native country. But unlike Wright with his flamboyant personality and Le Corbusier, who had always enjoyed the role of a rebel, Mies van der Rohe remained the retiring, modest person he had always been, living simply in his Chicago apartment surrounded by his collection of Klee paintings, listening to classical music, and reading German philosophers. Yet the impact of his architecture was felt throughout the world and remained important even after his death a decade ago in 1969.

The two most famous painters of the twentieth century, Matisse and Picasso, are discussed in other sections of this book, but there are several other leading members of the School of Paris who should be mentioned. Notable among them is Georges Braque, who lived from 1882 to 1963, dying at the age of eighty-one. Although he probably made his most significant contributions to modern art during his younger days, he continued working at a very high level of excellence to the end of his life. Outstanding among his later works are the still lifes he painted during the Second World War, which created a sensation when they were first shown in Paris and led to his receiving the Grand Prix in the Venice Biennale in 1948, when he was sixty-six years old. Other remarkable paintings of his old age are the series of pictures of his studio and those of birds produced during the 1950s and the murals he did for the Louvre and the Foundation Maeght at St. Paul de Vence. As an old man, he also took up lithography and sculpture and produced masterpieces in these media as well.

A similar vigor and creativity in old age is evident in the work of his contemporary, Fernand Léger, who was born in 1881 and died at the age of seventy-four in 1955. He too had been one of the pioneers of the modern art movement and had produced some of his

*Georges Braque*
The Wash Stand
*1944*
*Courtesy The Phillips Collection,*
*Washington, D.C.*

*Georges Braque was sixty-three when he*
*painted* The Wash Stand *in 1944.*

best work as a young man, but continued to be artistically active to the time of his death. The war years, during which he was in his early sixties, were spent in the United States, where he painted some fine landscapes and figure paintings, but he returned to France in 1945. During the next ten years he produced large canvases of workers, builders, divers, acrobats, and cyclists that combined Cubist aesthetics with more representational subject matter and showed him at the height of his power. *The Builders* of 1950, now in

*Fernand Léger*
The Great Parade
*1954*
*Courtesy Collection The Solomon R. Guggenheim Museum,*
*New York*

The Great Parade *was painted in 1954 when the seventy-three-year-old Léger*
*was at the height of his power.*

the Musée Léger, and the *Grande Parade* of 1953, now in The
Solomon R. Guggenheim Museum, are characteristic of this phase
of his career. A man of prodigious energy, Léger painted murals,
designed stained-glass windows and tapestries, made sets for the-
aters, produced mosaics, and made polychrome ceramic sculptures,
an activity that he continued into the seventh decade of his life.

A third French painter of this generation who lived a long and
fruitful life was Georges Rouault, who was born in 1871 and died in
1958 at the age of eighty-seven. A very devout man, many of whose
pictures are devoted to religious subjects, he has often been referred
to as the greatest religious painter of the twentieth century. While
the output of his later years is probably not on quite the same level
as that of his youth, he continued to produce important work
throughout the 1930s and the 1940s, and even such a late picture
as the *Christian Nocturn* of 1952, painted when he was eighty-one

and now in the collection of the Musée National d'Art Moderne in Paris, shows him still in full command of his powers. In addition to his oil paintings, Rouault also designed stained-glass windows for the church at Assy, tapestries for commercial reproduction, and numerous prints, of which the *Passion* and *Clown* series of 1948 are the finest.

Another Expressionist painter who continued working into old age was the German artist Emil Nolde. He was born as Emil Hansen in the village of Nolde in 1867 and died not far from there in Seebüll in Holstein in 1956, on the eve of his ninetieth birthday. His artistic development was rather slow, for he emerged as a major artist only in the early twentieth century when he was already forty, but after that he became one of the most creative and important figures in modern German painting. His output was enormous; he worked in oil but also was particularly outstanding as a painter of watercolors and as a printmaker. Although he was forbidden to work during the Hitler period, this did not stop him, for he created small sketches, which he called "forbidden" pictures, and later reworked them into larger ones. Although he was already close to eighty when, after the end of the war, he was permitted to exhibit again, he resumed work with undiminished power. As H. H. Arnason says, "The last self-portrait, done in 1947 when he was eighty, is painted with a forceful brushstroke that seems to have lost none of its vigor with age."[28]

Other twentieth-century artists who continued to be productive in their old age were the great pioneers of abstract painting, the Russian Wassily Kandinsky and the Dutchman Piet Mondrian. Kandinsky, who was the elder of the two, was born in Russia in 1866 and died in France at the age of seventy-eight in 1944. His work can be divided into three major periods, an early one when he was associated with the Blue Rider group in Munich, a middle one when he taught at the Bauhaus, and a late one when he lived in Paris. This last phase

[28] Arnason, *History*, p. 165.

*Wassily Kandinsky*
Ribbon with Squares, No. 731
*1944*
*Courtesy Collection The Solomon R. Guggenheim Museum, New York*

Ribbon with Squares, No. 731 *is one of Kandinsky's last works. It was painted in 1944, the year of his death at seventy-eight.*

started in 1933, when he was sixty-seven years old, and continued to the time of his death. Stimulated by the artistic atmosphere of the French capital and his close association with artists such as Miró and Arp, Kandinsky developed a new style of abstract painting that was related to organic and biomorphic forms rather than the rigorous geometric ones he had employed earlier. Werner Haftmann describes his pictures in these words: "Consummate mastery of the resources of Western painting, Byzantine splendor of color, the richest imagination, coolness of presentation, the freest intuition, and clearest intellectual control, are combined to produce a magnificent synthesis which once again enables him to fill concrete forms with intimate human meanings."[29]

Mondrian, born in 1872, six years after Kandinsky, died in 1944, the same year as the Russian artist. Mondrian's late period, starting with his move to London in 1938, when he was sixty-six,

[29] Werner Haftmann, *Painting in the Twentieth Century*, vol. 1 (New York: Praeger, 1966), p. 248.

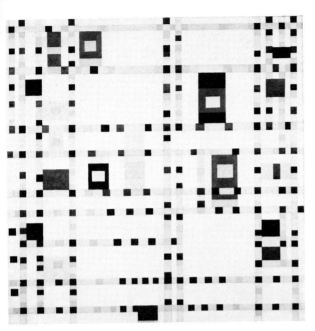

*Piet Mondrian*
Broadway Boogie-Woogie
*1942–1943*
*Courtesy Collection, The*
*Museum of Modern Art,*
*Given anonymously,*
*New York*

*Many critics consider Mondrian's*
Broadway Boogie-Woogie *of*
*1942–1943 to be his single most*
*accomplished painting. The*
*artist was seventy when he*
*painted it.*

and developing even more fruitfully in the United States, where he stayed during the war years, are by common consent considered one of the most creative times in his artistic career. Although he had only a few years left, this was a period of great joy and creativity when he produced some of his greatest masterpieces, such as *Trafalgar Square* of 1939 to 1943 and above all, *Broadway Boogie-Woogie* of 1942 to 1943, now in The Museum of Modern Art in New York and regarded by many critics as his single most accomplished painting. The spirit of the big city and of jazz music, of which he was very fond, inspired him to develop a new and vigorous manner that enabled him to produce some of his finest and most satisfying work when he was a man of seventy and within a few years of his death.

In the United States several of the leading figures of twentieth-century painting lived into their eighties and produced some of their best works during old age. Among the more traditional artists, the most outstanding was Edward Hopper, who was born in 1882 and died at age eighty-five in 1967. A very American artist who, as he once put it, gave expression to ". . . the chaos of ugliness . . . our native architecture with its hideous beauty,"[30] he produced works

[30] George Hamilton, *19th and 20th Century Art* (New York: Abrams, 1970), p. 302.

*Edward Hopper*
Second-Story Sunlight
*1960*
*Courtesy Collection of Whitney Museum of American Art,*
*Gift of the Friends of the Whitney Museum of American Art, New York*

*Edward Hopper kept alive an older tradition of American painting, as is seen*
*in his* Second-Story Sunlight *of 1960, painted when he was seventy-eight.*

that evoke a great deal of nostalgia and are rendered in a simplified, almost abstract manner, in spite of the realism of his subject matter. Portraying the lonely all-night coffee shops, gas stations, cheap hotels, movie houses, and old-fashioned buildings of America, Hopper brings to life in his pictures something of the essential quality of the American scene. Continuing to work into his old age, he kept alive an older tradition of characteristically American painting. He was revered by conservatives and moderns alike and was honored with a large retrospective at the Whitney Museum of American Art in 1964, when he was eighty-two years old, and at the Biennale in Sao Paolo, Brazil.

Two American painters who worked in a more abstract idiom and lived to be eighty-five were Mark Tobey and Lyonel Feininger.

*Mark Tobey*
Mystery of the Light
*1969*
*Courtesy Collection of the Willard Gallery,*
*New York*

*Tobey painted* Mystery of the Light *in 1969, his seventy-ninth year.*

Tobey was born in Wisconsin in 1890 but spent most of his life in Seattle, moving to Switzerland only in his old age and dying there in 1976. A highly original and deeply spiritual artist who was steeped in Zen Buddhism and Bahai, Tobey was one of the pioneers of abstract painting in America. Using calligraphic forms, he painted a series of pictures he called *White Writing* whose intricate traceries anticipated Abstract Expressionism. In 1958, when he was sixty-eight years old, his work was singled out for the first prize at the Venice Biennale. He was active to the very end of his life, and John Russell, writing in *The New York Times*, said, "As a sick man in his 80's, he more than once manifested in large paintings, a sustained physical energy that astonished his admirers; and retained to the last a salty, uncompromising outlook on life that found outlet in many an unpublished drawing."[31]

31 John Russell, "Tobey, Abstract Artist, 85, Dies," *The New York Times*, April 25, 1973, p. 53.

*Lyonel Feininger*
Early Steamer
*c. 1955*
*Courtesy Collection of The Willard Gallery, New York*

*Feininger was eighty-four years old when he painted this highly*
*original, spontaneous work.*

Feininger was born in New York City in 1871 but spent most of his life in Germany, where he taught at the Bauhaus, then returning to his native country in 1936 after Hitler's rise to power. Although he was already sixty-five at the time, he started an entirely new phase of his artistic career during these American years and produced some of his most remarkable work. His output initially was rather small, but toward the very end of his life he experienced a burst of creative activity that resulted in a series of beautiful late pictures painted in a very colorful, spontaneous style in contrast to the more Cubist style of his earlier work. He died in 1956, at the age of eighty-five, after over fifty years of unbroken artistic creativity.

Another artist who for some years had worked at the Bauhaus was the German-born American painter, Joseph Albers, who lived from 1888 to 1976. A teacher and theoretician who had a lifelong interest in problems of light and color, he did not emerge as a major painter until late in life. His first one-man show was held in New York in 1949, when he was sixty-one, and it was really not until he was in his seventies that he was able to support himself by painting.

*Josef Albers*
Homage to the Square—Frontal Backing
*1970*
*Courtesy The Metropolitan Museum of Art,*
*Gift of Josef Albers, 1972, New York*

*From the 1950s until his death in 1976, Josef Albers devoted himself to a*
*series of paintings and prints entitled* Homage to the Square. *This work,*
Homage to the Square—Frontal Backing, *was painted in 1970 when Albers*
*was eighty-two.*

However, the geometric pictures of his late years established him as
a major figure in the American art scene not only as an artist but
also as a teacher at Yale University. George Hamilton, in discussing
his contribution to modern art, has this to say: "Albers' exhaustive
theoretical and practical studies of the structure of color perception,
disseminated by his teachings as well as by his own painting, have
been fundamental for the development not only of hard edge painting but of an art of optical perception or Op Art, as it has been
called for the past few years."[32] Beginning in the 1950s, Albers

[32] Hamilton, *19th and 20th Century*, p. 401.

devoted himself to a series of paintings and prints that he called *Homage to the Square*, works that embody his insights and artistic ideas and are today regarded as among the masterpieces of geometric abstract paintings.

In sculpture, too, several of the leading figures of the twentieth century led very long and productive lives. The earliest of these was Aristide Maillol, who was born in 1861. He had started his career as a painter and tapestry maker, but in 1898 took up sculpture and for the next four decades produced large bronze images of female nudes that are today regarded as among the finest of modern sculptures. Developing a distinctive style that combined Classicism with modern abstraction, he worked in this manner until the time of his death at eighty-three in 1944. Although he gave different names to these statues, such as *Pomona, La Nuit, Venus, Isle de France*, or just *Nude*, the theme remains the same, namely, the beauty and plasticity of the female body. Among the masterpieces of his old age are *The River* of 1939 to 1943, now in The Museum of Modern Art in New

*Aristide Maillol*
The River
*Begun 1938–1939, completed 1943*
*Courtesy Collection, Museum of Modern Art,*
*Mrs. Simon Guggenheim Fund, New York*

The River *of 1938–1943 was completed when Maillol was eighty-two.*

York, a work that he created when he was eighty years old. In addition to his sculpture, Maillol also illustrated books with wood-cuts, some of the best of which were produced when he was in his seventies.

A far more revolutionary figure was Constantin Brancusi who was born in Rumania in 1876 but lived most of his life in Paris, where he died in 1957 at the age of eighty-one. His artistic career was a very long one, spanning some five decades during which he produced a large number of masterpieces that have had a tremendous influence on all modern art. Some of his finest works were produced when he was in his seventies, such as the *King of Kings* of 1956, now in The Solomon R. Guggenheim Museum. In his sculptures, Brancusi goes back to timeless archetypes, forms that have haunted men throughout the ages, and renders them in the simple, abstract language of twentieth-century art. A consummate craftsman, he carved directly

*Constantin Brancusi*
King of Kings
*1937*
*Courtesy Collection The*
*Solomon R. Guggenheim*
*Museum, New York*

*Brancusi, a revolutionary figure*
*in modern sculpture, executed*
King of Kings *in 1937, his*
*sixty-first year.*

into stone or wood or used highly polished bronze or brass, achieving a kind of formal perfection rarely found in modern art. Active to the very end of his life, he enjoyed great fame as the leading and most influential figure in modern sculpture. Big retrospectives of his work were held at The Solomon R. Guggenheim Museum in 1955 on the eve of his eightieth birthday and in 1969 after his death.

Two other pioneers of modern abstract sculpture who lived to an advanced age were Jean, or Hans, Arp and Naum Gabo. The former was born at Strasbourg in the Alsace in 1887 and lived most of his life in France. He died in Basel in 1966 in his eightieth year. One of the founders of the Zurich Dadaist group and an early member of the Surrealist movement, Arp was an extremely original avant-garde artist who created some of the finest sculptures of our period. Employing organic shapes that remind one of human bodies, breasts, buttocks, shells, crystals, fruits, and buds, he evolved a very individual visual vocabulary, which at its best is really beautiful. Arp was active to the end of his long life, with some of the outstanding works of his old age being the *Constellation* of 1950, made for

*Hans Arp*
Seuil Configuration
*c. 1960*
*Courtesy The Metropolitan*
*Museum of Art,*
*Gift of Mr. and Mrs. Ralph F. Colin,*
*1976, New York*

*Hans Arp's* Seuil Configuration
*dates from late in the artist's*
*career. He died in 1966 at the*
*age of seventy-nine.*

the Harvard Graduate Center in Cambridge, the *Shepherd of the Clouds*, for the Plaza of the Cuidad Universitaria in Caracas in 1953, and the *A la suite de l'Unesco* relief sculpture of 1958–1959. In 1954, when he was sixty-eight, he received the sculpture prize at the Venice Biennale, and he was given retrospectives at The Museum of Modern Art in New York in 1958 and in Paris in 1962.

Naum Gabo was born in Briansk, Russia, in 1890. He studied and worked in Germany as a young man but, after a brief sojourn in France and ten years in England, he moved to the United States in 1946, where he died at eighty-seven in 1977. One of the founders of the Constructivist movement, Gabo was a teacher and writer as well as an artist and exerted a considerable influence on modern art. He thought of space as a structural part of the object and conceived of sculpture as mass situated in space. He remained creative to the very end and did some of his most interesting work when he was in his seventies and even eighties. Good examples of such late works are the "spheral" theme he made for Princeton University and the fountain for St. Thomas Hospital, which was unveiled in 1976, only a year before his death. A large retrospective was given to him at the Tate Gallery in London when he was eighty-six years old.

The most original and beloved of native twentieth-century American sculptors was Alexander Calder, who was born in Philadelphia in 1898 and died in New York City in 1976 at the age of seventy-eight. A great innovator who invented a type of moving sculpture known as mobiles and in later life produced monumental static sculptures that he called stabiles, Calder was the first American modernist who exerted world-wide influence. Especially during the last two decades of his life, honors and commissions came to him from all over the United States and abroad, and he undertook major assignments not only for New York, Chicago, and Grand Rapids, but Paris, Hanover, Spoleto, and Jerusalem as well as Japan and Australia. His artistic energy was so great that he produced a huge body of work, continuing to create almost to his dying day. Exhibitions of his work were held in all major art centers and proved immensely successful, notably the one at The Museum of Modern Art in New York in 1968 in honor of his seventieth birthday, and the one at the Whitney Museum of American Art in 1976, which opened only a few days before his death. Jean Lipman, who organized this show, called "Calder's Universe," had this to say after Calder's death: "He died at what was absolutely the peak of his career. A lot of artists live into old age and we're very kind about them but the fact is that Sandy's work was greater every year. *Universe*, the motorized mural he did in 1974 for the Sears Tower in Chicago, was the great culminating masterpiece of ideas he'd been working on for 50 years."[33]

Another important and influential American sculptor was the Russian-born Jacques Lipchitz, who lived from 1891 to 1973. During his earlier years he lived in Paris, where he was part of the Cubist movement. In 1941, when he was fifty, he came to America, where he spent most of his remaining years and died at eighty-one in 1973. It was during his American period that he developed his late style, one that broke away from the rather austere geometric shapes of his early work, moving toward a freer, more Baroque type of image. Hilton Kramer, in characterizing it, put it this way: "The later work, which includes a great many small spontaneous 'sketches' as well as large public sculptures for which Lipchitz has become famous and admired the world over, are executed in a kind of neo-Baroque expressionist style, forms to be read to be massive, rounded . . . there is an evident attempt to attain an exalted eloquence—an ambition to create a universal statement on an epic scale. The themes are drawn from Biblical and mythological sources."[34] Still absorbed in his work at the very end of his life, on his deathbed the eighty-one-year-old sculptor asked his wife to see that his last three projects were completed, a task to which his widow devoted herself faithfully. As a result, his thirty-three-foot-high bronze statue, *Government by the People* in Philadelphia; his largest work, the fifty-six-

[33] *New York Times* obituary, November 12, 1976.
[34] Hilton Kramer, "The Achievement of Jacques Lipchitz," *The New York Times*, June 10, 1973.

*Jacques Lipchitz*
Bellerophon Taming Pegasus
*1973*
*Columbia Law School, Columbia University, New York*

Bellerophon Taming Pegasus *was one of three projects brought to completion by Jacques Lipchitz's wife after his death at eighty-one in 1973.*

foot *Bellerophon*, designed for the Law School Library of Columbia University; and *The Tree of Life* for the Hadassah Hospital on Mount Scopus now stand as a living testimony to the creative power of the aged Lipchitz.

All the figures discussed in this chapter are now dead, but as this is being written there are many living artists in their seventies, eighties, or, in some cases, even nineties, who are still actively engaged in their artistic careers. Since they are still producing, it seems premature to assess their life's work at this time, but the names of some of the most outstanding should at least be mentioned. The two most famous are probably the Spanish painter Joan Miró and the British sculptor Henry Moore. Miró, although ninety, continues to be one of the most original and delightful artists of our age, and Moore at eighty-five still undertakes major sculptural commissions. Only one year younger are Rufino Tamayo, the greatest living Mexican painter, and Raphael Soyer, the grand old man of modern American Realists, who are both eighty-four. A contemporary of theirs is America's leading woman sculptor, Louise Nevelson, who was also born in 1899. At eighty-two Jean Dubuffet continues to be a highly original and very creative artist. Close in age and now nearing their eightieth birthdays are the famous Spanish Surrealist Salvador Dali, the Dutch born-American Abstract Expressionist Willem de Kooning and the Japanese-American sculptor Isamu Noguchi. Older than any of these and therefore discussed in the last chapter are the Russian-born French painter Marc Chagall and the grand old dame of American painting, Georgia O'Keeffe.

*Henry Moore*
*Reclining Figure*
*1963–1965*
*Photo Courtesy Lincoln Center for the Performing Arts, Inc.,*
*New York*

*Sculptor Henry Moore's large* Reclining Figure, *which graces Lincoln Center, was executed between 1963 and 1965, the artist's sixty-fifth to sixty-eighth years.*

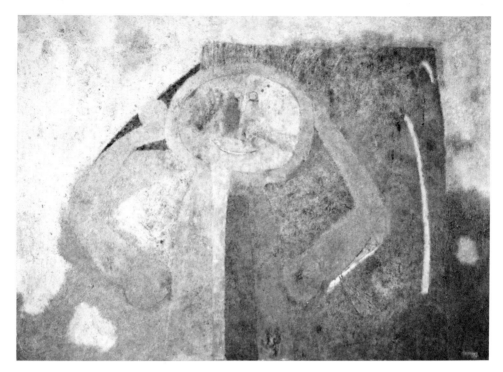

*Rufino Tamayo*
Hombre Sonriente
*1977*
*Courtesy Marlborough Gallery, New York*

Hombre Sonriente *by the Mexican painter Tamayo was produced in the*
*artist's seventy-eighth year.*

*Raphael Soyer*
Deborah
*1977*
*Courtesy Forum Gallery,*
*New York*

*Raphael Soyer painted this work,*
Deborah, *in 1977, at the age of*
*seventy-eight.*

# 5 PAST THE PEAK

*W*hile there have been many artists who continued to work on a very high level throughout their lives, there are others who, after a very creative early period, suffered a marked decline in their later years. As Degas once said, "Anyone can have talent when he is five and twenty, the thing is to have talent when you're fifty." This is certainly true, and the history of art, especially during the twentieth century, has numerous examples of artists who in their youth produced significant and original work only to lose their creative power and distinctive vision in later life. This is particularly true of those who were caught up in the excitement of the revolutionary decade of twentieth-century art between 1905 and 1914, when the Fauves, the Cubists, the Expressionists, the Futurists, and the early Surrealists were active and the air seemed to be charged with a creative energy never again encountered in the art of our century. Several of the young artists made important contributions at that time but were unable to maintain the inspired quality of their work despite the fact that some of them lived into their seventies or eighties and continued working to their dying day. Just when this decline sets in varies from person to person, depending upon the circumstances of their life such as their success or failure, their mental state, and many other factors. In the case of the two most noteworthy figures discussed in this chapter, de Chirico reached his climax at twenty-five and had spent himself by thirty, while Picasso poured out a wealth of magnificent creations until he was sixty, after which his work began to deteriorate.

No doubt in earlier periods many painters and sculptors produced their best work in their youth or middle age and lost some of their power as they grew old, but a marked decline at an early age is a relatively modern phenomenon that began with the Romantic movement.

The earliest of these artists was the English painter Samuel Palmer, who lived from 1805 to 1881. A very precocious youth, he exhibited his work at the Royal Academy for the first time in 1820, when he was only fifteen years old, and did his finest work, consisting of a series of sketchbooks produced from 1825 to 1835, between his twentieth and thirtieth years. A visionary and mystic who was profoundly influenced by Blake, Palmer painted small ink-and-wash sketches and a few oils, which depicted the Shoreham Valley of Kent in a highly original and powerful style. After his trip to Italy and his return to London, he had far greater commercial success, but he was never able to recapture the romantic vision of his early years. As Geoffrey Grigson said in his study of the artist, Palmer climbed "to a point of intuition and power as an artist which he never reached again in the forty-six years he had to live. But the dwindling and close of his effective, realized idealism needs to be clarified by showing what in fact he did become. Up to 1835, as I have said, the change was gradual, then, after his Devonshire journey, after his determination to struggle up into repute, the change of his style was quick and obvious although the clinching step did not take place until after his marriage in 1833 and his hard-working honeymoon visit to Italy." He concludes, "He was not an extraordinary artist after his early flaming died down to a glow."[1]

Far more important and tragic figures were the two late nineteenth- and early twentieth-century painters, James Ensor and

[1] Geoffrey Grigson, *Samuel Palmer* (London: Kegan Paul, 1947), p. x.

Edvard Munch. Both of them lived to be old men, but they did their most outstanding work in their youth and were never able to recapture the inspiration and intensity of their early work.

Ensor, a Flemish painter who lived most of his life in Ostend in Belgium, was a highly original artist who, when only in his twenties, produced pictures that made an important contribution to the Symbolist movement and anticipated Expressionism and Surrealism. A favorite motif was the use of masked figures, which appeared for the first time in a picture he called *Scandalized Masks*, which he painted in 1883 when he was only twenty-three years old. It is now in the Royal Museum of Fine Arts in Brussels. His most ambitious and famous work, *Christ's Entry into Brussels*, was painted six years later when he was at the end of his twenties. For about a decade after this he still produced some fine works, but after 1900 a decline set in that continued despite the recognition he received later and the baronry bestowed upon him in 1929. As his biographer Paul Haesaerts said, "Toward 1900, when the hostility against him began slowly to yield to admiration, Ensor, who had almost reached the mid-point of his life, who was in the prime of life, seemed to falter. . . . While he did not give up painting, and continued to draw and write, he was no longer the magnificent inventor, as individualistic, as fertile, as daring as he had been."[2] Whatever the reason for his decline—an inner failure of his earlier lack of recognition and inability to sell his work—he never again reached the greatness of his early period, although he lived another fifty years, dying in 1949 at the age of eighty-nine. During his last twenty years he was a bitter recluse, avoiding people and taking no interest in the art world in spite of the fact that he was now universally recognized as a great painter and much admired by other artists and critics.

Even more tragic was the life of the great Norwegian painter Edvard Munch, who was born in 1863, three years after Ensor, and died at the age of eighty-one in 1944. After studying in Oslo, he went to Paris in 1885, where he came under the influence of Toulouse-Lautrec, Gauguin, and Van Gogh, and then traveled in Germany, where he exhibited at the Verein Berliner Künstler in

[2] Paul Haesaerts, *Ensor* (New York: Abrams, 1959), p. 209.

1892 and the Berliner Sezession in 1902. It was during these years that he was most inspired, and along with Van Gogh and Gauguin, Munch became one of the germinal figures in the Expressionist movement. His woodcuts of the period, the first of which was made in 1896, when he was thirty-three, and his powerful and haunting paintings, notably the *Frieze of Life* series of 1897, 1903, and 1906, are among the most important and original of all early Expressionist paintings and had a great influence, especially on young German painters. But in 1908 when he was thirty-five years old, he suffered a nervous breakdown and spent seven months in a neurological clinic in Copenhagen. Unlike Van Gogh, who under similar circumstances and at approximately the same age committed suicide, Munch regained his health, but he had lost the intensity of his extraordinary artistic vision. Although he continued to paint, and some of his later work does have a certain merit, as Jean Selz says in his book on the artist, "If we look at Munch's entire output during his long development . . . we are obliged to say that everything in his painting that bears the mark of genius, that plunges into the dark recesses of the human being . . . was done before 1908."[3] Although he produced some of his most ambitious paintings after this date, there can be no doubt that the result was uninspired and represented a repetition of earlier themes in a less inventive and less expressive form. Toward the end of his life, Munch had to give up painting altogether because of failing eyesight, but by that time his genius had completely spent itself.

The most dramatic example of an artist who did his best work in his youth and led a long life during which he produced many more paintings, none of which equaled his early output, is Giorgio de Chirico. He was born in Greece of Italian parents in 1888 and studied in Greece and Munich. In 1911 at the age of twenty-three, he went to Paris, where he stayed until 1915, when he had to return to his native country to join the army. It was during the five years between his twenty-third and twenty-seventh years that he produced dream landscapes—the pictures that earned him the reputation of

[3] Jean Selz, *Edvard Munch* (New York: Crown, 1974), p. 76.

being one of the great masters of modern art. These paintings, which combine beauty of classical forms with a surreal atmosphere that gives them a haunting quality, established the young artist as one of the most gifted pioneers of twentieth-century painting.

After this brief florescence, de Chirico's artistic power began to decline during his next phase when, together with his friend Carlo Carra, he founded the Pittura Metafisica group. In 1918 at the age of thirty he turned to Romantic Classicism and his art lost its great originality and intensity of vision. Although he continued working right through his eighties, and only died at ninety in 1978, none of the later pictures have any really outstanding merit, for as Keith Roberts said in reviewing a recent exhibition, "His late painting style does not suit his imagery because it weakens the vital note of objectivity, a sense of dreams calmly set down by the clear light of day."[4] The tragic fact that everyone admired what he had done in his twenties but had no use for the artistic output of his maturity and old age ". . . led to de Chirico's evident conviction that he was the centre of the universe and that everyone else, especially the critics and other painters, was subsidiary, stupid and hostile towards him."[5]

A similar decline may be observed in the careers of two other Italian painters of his generation, Giacomo Balla and Carlo Carra. Both lived to be very old and remained artistically active into their eighties, but neither produced any significant works during the second half of his life. Balla, who was the elder of the two, was born in Turin in 1871 and died in Rome in 1958. He studied in Paris around the turn of the century and became interested in Neo-Impressionism, but it was not until 1910, after founding Futurism with Severini and Boccione, that he emerged as an important artist. Works such as *Dog on a Leash* show him a delightful and original painter. But with the death of Boccione in 1916, Futurism lost its vitality. Balla joined

[4] Keith Roberts, "Current-Forthcoming Exhibitions," *Burlington* magazine, May 1976.
[5] M. Crosland, Introduction to the *Memoirs of Giorgio de Chirico* (London: Peter Owen, 1971), p. 9.

the Metaphysical school and by 1930, he had returned to more traditional painting, executing a large number of pictures that lack any originality or distinction. He died at the age of eighty-seven, having ceased for more than a generation to play any significant role in modern art.

The somewhat younger Carra was born in 1881, the same year as Picasso and Léger, and died at eighty-five in 1966. Like so many young artists of that period, he gravitated to Paris, which he first visited in 1900 and to which he returned for a longer stay in 1911. One of the founders of the Futurist movement whose manifesto he signed in 1910, Carra was a highly original and very creative artist. In 1917, when he was in the army, he met de Chirico, with whom he founded the Metaphysical school of painting. By 1919 when he was only thirty-eight years old, he, too, returned to a more conventional mode of painting under the impact of having studied Giotto and Masaccio. Although he continued to paint and had a great influence on a younger generation of Italian artists as a teacher at the Milan Art Academy, his later pictures, while pleasing enough, had none of the imaginative power or inventiveness that the work of his late twenties and early thirties had possessed.

In the school of Paris, this tendency to decline after a brilliant early period is less pronounced, with most of the great masters, such as Matisse, Picasso, Braque, Léger, and Rouault, producing outstanding works well into their maturity and even old age. But here, too, some of the lesser artists who were carried along by the surge of creative activity during the early years of the century could not sustain their momentum and lost much of their expressive power during their later years. This was particularly true of some of the members of the Fauve group, notably Andre Derain and Maurice de Vlaminck, who had helped found this movement and were among its most gifted exponents. While both continued to paint and enjoyed a good deal of success in later years, it was when they were in their twenties that they produced their most original and aesthetically successful canvases.

Vlaminck, who was born in Paris in 1876 and died at the age of eighty-two in 1958, had started life as a racing cyclist and was a self-taught painter. It was only after he met Derain and Matisse in 1901 and discovered Van Gogh, who deeply impressed him, that he turned seriously to painting. His work was shown at the First Fauve Exhibition of 1905. Vlaminck's art of those years had an explosive quality that made it quite remarkable, but in 1908 he became interested in the work of Cézanne, and for the rest of his life he painted brooding landscapes in dark tonalities that, while accomplished, had none of the power of his early work.

Derain, who was closely associated with Vlaminck and actually lived with him at Chatou from 1901 to 1902, had a similar career. Born in 1880, he joined the Fauves when he was in his early twenties and became one of the most powerful and creative artists in the group. However, in 1908 he discovered Cézanne and became a Cubist, which proved less congenial to his gifts. By 1920 he had turned to a more academic, classical type of art, and while he painted many beautiful landscapes, nudes, and still lifes even in his later years, he never again achieved the dynamic energy and expressive power that characterized his early work. He died at seventy-four in 1954.

Another French artist of the same generation who experienced a marked decline in his later years was Maurice Utrillo. Born in 1883, he died at the age of seventy-two in 1955. His early pictures, which represent street scenes from the Montmartre district of Paris, have a lyrical beauty all their own. Painted in light tonalities with much use of white and rendered in a semiabstract style, they evoke the charm of the streets and houses of this section of Paris in a very lovely way and are among the most attractive pictures that were painted there at the time. But by the mid-1920s a tragic change had occurred, for Utrillo had become an alcoholic and in 1924, when he was forty years old, he tried to commit suicide in a police station. After that his mother, Suzanne Valadon, took him to a castle in southern France, where she supervised him closely and set him to work every day painting pictures from postcards of Paris. Then, as H. H. Arnason says, "From 1930 until his death in 1955, Utrillo, now decorated with the Legion of Honor, lived at Le Vesmet outside of Paris, where his wife watched over him carefully, and he divided his time between painting and religious devotions. During these twenty-five years of rectitude, he did little but repeat his earlier paintings."[6] Another French painter who, in spite of a spectacular start, never developed into a major artist was Francis Picabia, who lived from 1878 to 1953. One of the pioneers of twentieth-century art who had belonged to most of the avant-garde movements of his day, first Cubism, then Section d'Or, of which he was the founder, later Dadaism, and finally Surrealism, Picabia was in the forefront of the revolutionary phase of modern art during the first quarter of the century. He was a leading figure in the Armory Show of 1913 that introduced modern art to America, and he was a friend of Alfred Stieglitz, who was the first to show the great artists of the twentieth century in New York. A man who loved polemics, Picabia thrived on controversy and participated in every battle modern art had to fight. While producing no work comparable to the best paintings of his great contemporaries, he nevertheless represented a vital force on the modern art scene. With his sense of the absurd and the ridiculous, it was probably Dadaism that proved most congenial to him, and it was in this vein that he produced his best work. However, in 1926 when he was forty-eight years old, he took up representational painting and abandoned the more experimental style of his younger years. In 1945, toward the end of his life, he returned to abstract art, but his really creative period had occurred many years before when he was still a young man.

Even more striking is the case of the leading Czech painter, Frank, or Franz, Kupka, who was born in 1871 and died at eighty-six in 1957. After studying in Prague and Vienna, he moved to Paris in 1895, when he was twenty-five years old, and it was here that he spent most of his life. A pioneer Abstractionist, in 1911 he founded

[6] H. Horvard Arnason, *History of Modern Art* (New York: Prentice-Hall, 1968), p. 279.

the Orphist group with Robert Delaunay and painted some of the earliest completely abstract paintings. While he continued to adhere to the principles of nonobjective painting throughout his life and was one of the leading members of the Abstraction-Creation group, his most important work was done between 1910 and 1920, from his fortieth to his fiftieth years. His later pictures, influenced by Mondrian and Neo-Plasticism, became more geometric in style. This work, because of the change of taste, found little acclaim during the 1920s and 1930s, and it was not until the postwar period, when there was a renewed interest in abstract painting, that Kupka once again came to the forefront and his early work was rediscovered. In 1946 a big show of his work was held in his native country at which the government bought fifty of his paintings to be placed in the Kupka Museum in Prague; and in 1958, the year after his death, a large retrospective of his work was held at the Musée National de l'Art Moderne in Paris and at The Museum of Modern Art in New York.

The same phenomenon that occurred in France also happened in German twentieth-century painting. The leading figures, such as Nolde, Klee, Kirchner, and Beckmann, continued to produce excellent works throughout their lives, while the second-rank artists who had participated in the revolutionary phase of modern German art suffered a decline once the élan of the original inspiration had spent itself. Typical of this development were three members of the Brücke group, which had been founded in 1905. All three were born in the 1880s, came to artistic maturity during the first decade of the twentieth century, and lived into old age, but their significant contribution to Expressionism was made during their youth before the breakup of the Brücke in 1913 and the onset of the First World War the following year.

The eldest of the three was Max Pechstein, who was born in 1881 and died in 1955 at the age of seventy-six. A founding member of the Brücke along with Heckel and Kirchner, he was one of the most vital and expressive of German artists of the decade between 1905 and 1914, but after his appointment to the faculty of the Berlin Academy of Art and his election to the Prussian Art Academy in 1919, his painting showed a decline in its artistic power. As Peter Selz says, "After 1914 his work lost much of its former interest and strength, possibly because of its loss of tension. Pechstein became calmer, less eager to startle the common citizen; yet the robustness, the sensual quality, and the expression of his own vital energy were also lost in his later productions. Frequently he turned to stylized decoration."[7] During the Nazi period, his work was suppressed because it was considered degenerate and in 1945, at the end of the war, when Pechstein was restored to his former position and was overwhelmed with honors, he was unable to recapture the expressive power that his youthful work had possessed.

His friend and cofounder of the Brücke, Erich Heckel, underwent a similar development. Born in 1883, he was in his early twenties when he emerged as one of the most interesting and revolutionary artists of the pre–World War One epoch, with oils and woodcuts that are justly regarded as among the strongest art produced in Germany at that time. But he too lost much of his power after serving in the medical corps of the German army from 1915 to 1918. By the 1920s, when he was in his late thirties, his creativity began to ebb. As Bernard Myers says, "Turning away from Expressionism in the twenties . . . Heckel's art became increasingly decorative and Fauve. . . . The same general development was true for his graphic works, which also became less and less emotive or psychologically stirring. Yet through the period of the First World War, both as a painter and graphic artist, Heckel was one of the most important artists in the Expressionist movement."[8] Although Heckel lived into old age, dying in 1970 at the age of eighty-seven, he never regained his prominent position nor did he produce works in any way comparable to those of his early period.

A similar fate befell the third member of this group, Karl Schmidt-Rottluff, who was born in 1884. While still a very young man, he became a member of the Brücke and produced a large number of paintings and especially prints. In his youth a powerful Expressionist artist and an associate of Nolde and Kirchner, he

[7] Peter Selz, *German Expressionist Painting* (Berkeley: University of California Press, 1957), p. 292.
[8] Bernard Myers, *The German Expressionists* (New York: McGraw-Hill, 1963), p. 127.

turned to a more naturalistic style during the 1920s and his work lost much of its vitality. With the advent of Hitler he was expelled from the Prussian Art Academy and forbidden to paint, but after the war he was restored to his former position and appointed professor of painting at the Berlin Art Academy. As the last survivor of the heroic age of modern German art, he was honored and celebrated at the end of his life but he never again produced any work that had the expressive power of his youthful art. He died at ninety-one in 1976 and left his work to the Brücke Museum in Berlin.

Two other German artists whose most fruitful period came in their early years were Otto Dix and George Grosz. Born in 1891 and 1893 respectively, they belong to a different generation from the Expressionists and came to artistic maturity in the post–World War One period. Dismayed by the horror and senselessness of the Great War and the chaotic conditions in Germany that followed it, they expressed their revulsion through their art, which gave it a bitterness and intensity that makes their work extremely powerful. During the 1920s, however, they turned to a very precise, realistic kind of art known as Neue Sachlichkeit or New Objectivity. Since they were politically active on the side of the socially conscious forces of the left, both were persecuted during the Nazi period, and Grosz settled in America in 1933, while Dix stayed in Germany and participated in an attempt on Hitler's life in 1939. By this time, however, neither was creating any significant art, nor did the end of the war bring any renewal of real creativity. In fact, Grosz, who had been one of the harshest and most brilliant of the social satirists during the years of the Weimar Republic, lost his bite after coming to the United States and turned to painting rather conventional nudes and landscapes of no great artistic distinction. He died at sixty-six in 1959 shortly after returning to his native country. Dix, who outlived him by a decade, died in 1969 at the age of seventy-eight. During his later years he produced a romantic type of painting based on German sixteenth-century masters such as Cranach and Altdorfer. After World War Two he turned more and more to religious and allegorical subjects, painting large pictures in an Expressionist style as well as portraits and still lifes. None of these works have the power or discipline of his earlier production, and they add little to his reputation, which will rest on the realistic paintings of the 1920s, done when he was a man in his thirties at the height of his artistic power.

In the United States there were several artists who made an important contribution in their youth and produced little of consequence in their later years. Outstanding among them are Morgan Russell and Stanton Macdonald-Wright. Russell, who was the older, was born in New York in 1886 and studied with Robert Henri. In 1906, when he was twenty years old, he moved to Paris, where he was exposed to the avant-garde tendencies of the day and met Macdonald-Wright, with whom he founded the Synchronist movement in 1912. A pioneer among American abstract painters, Russell participated in the Armory Show of 1913 and exhibited his work in Paris and Munich. However, in 1919, when he was thirty-three years old, he turned to representational art and never again produced anything as significant or aesthetically satisfying as the work of his youth. He returned to America in 1946 and died in 1953 at the age of sixty-six.

Macdonald-Wright was somewhat younger. Born in Virginia in 1890, he outlived Russell by twenty years, dying in 1973 at the age of eighty-three. He too went to Paris as a youth in 1907, and at the age of twenty-two emerged as one of the important avant-garde American artists. But unlike his friend Russell, he did not stay in Paris but returned to America in 1916. In 1919 he gave up Synchronism and began producing a more conventional type of painting. In his later years he became very interested in Oriental philosophy and visited Japan in order to study Zen Buddhism. He also taught Oriental art and aesthetics at the University of California in Los Angeles. In 1954, when he was sixty-four, he returned to abstract painting and had a large retrospective at the Los Angeles County Museum in 1956. However, the abstract work of his old age lacked the expressive power and inventiveness of that of his early years, for he too was at the height of his creativity when he was a young man in his twenties.

Other American artists who did their best work during the first half of their lives were the Russian-born painter Max Weber and the Ukrainian-born sculptor Alexander Archipenko. Weber, who came to America as a child and settled in Brooklyn, studied at the Pratt Institute and taught art in public schools. However, in 1905, when he was twenty-four, he went to Paris, where he met and became friendly with Matisse, Picasso, Delaunay, and Henri Rousseau. Under the impact of these encounters, he took up avant-garde art and became one of the pioneers of modern art in America. Although he returned to New York in 1908, he continued to keep in touch with the school of Paris and exhibited at the Bernheim-Jeune Gallery in 1924. An innovator who belonged to the "291" circle and reflected the influence of Fauvism and Cubism in his early work, Weber took up a more representational style in the 1920s, depicting landscapes, figures, and flowers. After 1940, he turned increasingly to Jewish subjects such as Hasidic dances, musicians, and religious scenes painted in an Expressionist style. Although he had considerable success with these pictures and was honored with a retrospective at the Whitney Museum of American Art in 1949, there is little doubt that it was during his early period that he made his greatest contribution to modern art. He died at eighty in 1961.

Archipenko, who was born in Kiev in 1887 and studied there and in Moscow, went to Paris in 1908 when he was twenty-one years old. There he encountered Cubism and developed into one of the most original and powerful of early Cubist sculptors. The works he produced between 1908 and 1920 show him at his high point, and are among the most important avant-garde sculptures of the twentieth century. However, he too gravitated increasingly to more traditional forms and after moving to the United States in 1923 at the age of thirty-six, lost much of his power and originality. Although active to the time of his death at seventy-seven in 1964 and an influential teacher who had his own art school, Archipenko never regained the excellence of his early work, and it is on the sculpture he produced during his twenties and early thirties that his fame as a major modern figure rests.

Pablo Picasso, the last of the artists to be dealt with in this category, is, of course, far more significant than any of the other artists discussed in this chapter. In fact, in the eyes of most critics he is the greatest and most influential painter of the twentieth century. The scope of his work alone, which moved from the Realism of his earliest painting to Impressionism, followed by the Romanticism of his Blue and Rose periods, the Expressionism of his African period, the revolutionary impact of his Cubist period counteracted by his Classical phase, which in turn was followed by a Surrealist period and ended in the social commentary of his *Guernica* and war pictures, would make him a major artist by any standards. The sheer volume of his output, comprising thousands of canvases as well as sculptures of great power and originality in addition to magnificent prints and drawings, is overwhelming and surpasses that of any other artist of his period. Equally impressive was his vitality, and when he died at the age of ninety-one in 1973, after an artistic career that spanned seventy-five years, he was still working like a man obsessed, producing when he was in his eighties no less than three canvases in an afternoon[9] and continuing to work to the day of his death. The output of his late years was greeted with great acclaim and spawned a whole Picasso literature in which entire volumes were devoted to the production of one single year of his life, such as *Picasso at Ninety*. Other works dealt with Picasso in his studio, Picasso's models, and many similar subjects, amounting to an endless stream of books, articles, and catalogs that seemed to suggest that he could do no wrong. However, as the years went by, critics began to question the validity of his late production. Younger artists, who at one time had hailed him as their master, no longer were interested in his current work, which, as Hilton Kramer once said, went from his villa at the Riviera to the elegant apartments on Park Avenue without making any impact on the art scene.

The British critic John Berger probably put it most succinctly in his 1965 book *The Success and Failure of Picasso*, in which the artist's late work was for the first time assessed and compared to the late work of other great artists:

[9] H. Parmelin, *Picasso, the Artist and His Model* (New York: Abrams, 1965), p. 66.

Painters unlike a certain kind of poet, need time to develop and slowly uncover their genius. There is not, I think, a single example of a great painter or sculptor whose work has not gained in profundity and originality as he grew older. Bellini, Michelangelo, Titian, Tintoretto, Poussin, Rembrandt, Goya, Turner, Degas, Cézanne, Monet, Matisse, Braque, all produced some of their very greatest works when they were over sixty-five. It is as though a lifetime is needed to master the medium, and only when the mastery had been achieved can an artist be simply himself, revealing the true nature of his imagination.

However favorably one judges Picasso's work since 1945, it cannot be said to show any advance on what he created before. To me, it represents a decline, a retreat, as I have tried to show, into an idealized and sentimental pantheism.[10]

This more severe judgment of the work of Picasso's last three decades is by no means unique but is shared by several other leading critics, such as Clement Greenberg, who, in assessing the artist's work in connection with the large Museum of Modern Art show of 1957, comes to the conclusion that *Guernica* was the last major turning point in Picasso's artistic development and that the artist's crisis, which as he sees it, set in in 1928, deepened after 1938. As he says, "Picasso continued to paint successful pictures, and with much greater frequency after 1938 than in the ten years before, but the paradox is explained by the lowering of the terms of his success after 1938. Since then he has also painted many, many very bad pictures, many more of them, and much worse, than the well-chosen Museum show would suggest."[11]

The tendency that Greenberg refers to became more and more pronounced as Picasso grew older, and during the last decade of his life, even by lower standards the artist's output lacked any real merit. Increasingly his paintings became variations on themes done far more successfully by Picasso himself in earlier years or by other painters such as Velázquez, Poussin, Delacroix, and Matisse. As Berger says, "They are no more than exercises in painting such as

[10] John Berger, *The Success and Failure of Picasso* (London: Pantheon, 1965), p. 181.
[11] Ibid., p. 183.

one might expect a serious young man to carry out, but not an old man who has gained the freedom to be himself."[12] The tension and expressive power are no longer present, having given way at best to a decorative playfulness that may be pleasing at times but lacks the quality of his earlier work. As John Russell put it in his obituary of the artist in *The New York Times*, "The content of the late Picasso is for the most part thin and self-preoccupied, the manner garrulous."

Considering the towering strength of his genius, this may appear to be a harsh judgment but now that the overpowering presence of the artist has vanished, this view is shared by an increasing number of critics and scholars. It seems almost as if the extraordinary fame and success that Picasso enjoyed after the Second World War, when his name became a household word and his every sketch and doodle was seized upon by eager dealers and undiscriminating collectors, undermined his sense of quality and of self-criticism. As more and more works of all kinds poured out of his studio, their aesthetic quality grew more and more feeble so that in the end hardly anything of real merit emerged, and the aged artist became a victim of his own facility and fame. If this fate could have been avoided, had Picasso been less idolized, less a public figure whose villa in Nice became a Mecca for dealers, museum directors, collectors, photographers, filmmakers, and all kinds of dubious hangers-on, we will never know, but there can be little doubt that all this did not help either Picasso or his art and that by the time of his death, his truly creative period had long passed.

12 Ibid., p. 185.

# 6 ENOUGH IS ENOUGH

*A*nother category of artists is composed of those who, although reaching old age, had for some reason given up working long before their death. The most dramatic and interesting of these is no doubt Marcel Duchamp, who lived from 1887 to 1968. A gifted and highly original artist, Duchamp started his artistic career as a Fauve but did not find his true style until he joined the Cubists in 1910, when he was twenty-three years old. In 1912, at the age of twenty-five, he painted his masterpiece, *Nude Descending a Staircase*, shown at the 1913 New York Armory Show, where it created a sensation and became the best-known modern painting in America. But Duchamp soon abandoned Cubism and turned to what he called "ready-mades," such as the wall urinal that he exhibited turned upside down and other objects taken from daily life. He also became a member of the Dadaist group, which proclaimed that it was against all art. As John Golding said, "Duchamp saw 1912 as the year in which he rejected the role of professional artist. The first version of the *Chocolate Grinder* of the following year witnessed his last essay in traditional techniques (with the exception of *Tu m'* of 1918, a commissioned work about which Duchamp later expressed doubts) and soon after came his first experiments on glass. By 1914 the plans for the *Large Glass* were all finalized so that the long labor involved in its execution in a sense qualified Duchamp for the simple role of 'artisan' which he was to claim."[1] This last work occupied him from 1915 to 1923 and became well known under the title *The Bride Stripped Bare by her Bachelors, Even* and was widely acclaimed by the artists of the Surrealist movement and by the Neo-Dadaist school of recent years.

With the completion of this work Duchamp, now thirty-six, largely gave up art and devoted most of his time to playing chess, although he remained associated with the Surrealists and created a coal-sack ceiling for the great 1938 International Surrealist Exhibition in Paris and a *Rain Room* for the Surrealist Show of 1947. It was also revealed at the time of his death that he had been working secretly on another major work, the *Etant Donnés*, produced between 1946 and 1966, in his sixties and seventies. It is a strange and baffling work related to *The Bride Stripped Bare by her Bachelors, Even*, and exists in a realm outside of conventional art. Both these assemblages are today installed in the Philadelphia Museum of Art. Yet even though this late tableau was discovered after his death at eighty-one, it is still true that the artist, who at an early age enjoyed great success and was very productive, stopped painting at twenty-five and virtually ended his artistic career at thirty-six.

A vast literature, which is steadily growing, deals with the phenomenon of Marcel Duchamp, and the artist himself contributed to it by giving interviews and writing about his art, life, and philosophy, often in a very contradictory way. In one such interview he said, "I consider painting as a means of expression, not as an end in itself. One means of expression among others, and not a complete end for life at all; in the same way I consider that color is only a means of expression in painting and not an end. In other words, painting should not be exclusively retinal or visual; it should have to do with the gray matter, with our urge for understanding. This is generally what I love. I didn't want to pin myself down to one little

[1] John Golding, *Marcel Duchamp, the Bride Stripped Bare by her Bachelors* (London: Allen Lane, 1971), p. 94.

circle, and I tried at least to be as universal as I could. That is why I took up chess."[2]

Other artists gave up working because they had little success or became involved in other fields. A notable example of the former was the American painter Louis Eilshemius, who lived from 1864 to 1941. Although he lived to the age of seventy-seven, he stopped painting at fifty-seven, having become discouraged because of his lack of recognition. An eccentric but highly gifted person, he produced a large body of work. In addition to his painting, he also wrote, composed music, and worked on various inventions. His paintings were romantic evocations of landscapes and mythological scenes executed in a visionary, highly personal style quite unlike anything else that was being produced at the time. Ironically enough, only after he had given up painting and had become a very embittered and somewhat mad old man did he receive belated recognition, for the Valentine Dudensing Gallery in New York gave him exhibitions in 1932 and 1933, and he also had a major show in Paris at the Durand-Rouel Gallery.

In the case of Charles Willson Peale, who was born in 1741, that he more or less gave up painting and turned to establishing the first important museum in the United States was at least partially due to the fact that the type of rather crude portrait painting he practiced was no longer popular in America. As his biographer James Thomas Flexner says,

> Undoubtedly Peale was driven into such activities as medical speculation by a growing sense of inferiority concerning his painting. As we have seen, he had never emerged from the unsophisticated tradition of his colonial predecessors, but during the revolutionary period all American painters had worked in this vein, and he had been outstanding among them. The return

[2] M. San Ouillet and E. Peterson, eds., *Salt Seller—The Writings of Marcel Duchamp (Marchand du Sel)* (New York: Oxford, 1973), pp. 135-136.

of prosperity brought to this country, however, such expert European trained artists as Gilbert Stuart, who settled in Philadelphia in 1794. . . . Lamenting the thousand interests that had kept him from sticking to his art when a young man, Peale announced his retirement from painting.[3]

In 1786, when he was fifty-five years old, he announced in the Pennsylvania *Packet* that he would make part of his house a repository of natural curiosities, and although he continued to produce some pictures even after this date, the major focus of his activity shifted from art to science and the accumulation of items for his museum, which became the most outstanding public display of objects that illustrated natural history, curiosities, artifacts of all kinds, and works of art in the United States. He continued managing the museum until his seventieth year and died at eighty-six in 1827.

Another outstanding person who gave up his artistic endeavors long before his death was the French engineer Alexandre Gustave Eiffel. Born in 1832, he had achieved great fame as an architect of the Eiffel Tower, erected for the Paris World Exposition of 1889. It is probably to this day the best-known edifice in all Paris. As Siegfried Giedion says, "The one-thousand-foot Eiffel Tower, erected for the Paris Exposition of 1889, embodied in a single work all his experience with foundations and supports against the intricacies of earth and wind. Even Eiffel himself was at first afraid to shock the ruling taste with the creation of an uncompromising bare structure in the heart of Paris."[4] In 1900, at the age of sixty-seven, Eiffel published a monumental book on the great work. Called *La Tour de trois cents metres* in it he refers to the tower as the personification of ". . . the art of the modern engineer and the century of industry and science." However, in 1912 when he was a man of seventy, he turned from the construction of bridges and viaducts, which had

---

[3] James T. Flexner, *America's Old Masters* (New York: Doubleday, 1967), p. 221.
[4] Siegfried Giedion, *Space, Time and Architecture*, 5th ed. (Cambridge: Harvard University Press, 1967), p. 281.

been his specialty, to aerodynamics. In 1911 he built the first wind tunnel to meet the needs of the aircraft industry, and in 1918 he tested the first airplane in a wind tunnel. In 1913 he also published a book, *Resistence of Air*, which was translated into English and had a great influence on the fledgling aeronautical industry. He died at ninety-one in 1923 after a long and extremely fruitful career as an engineer, architect, writer, and scientist—a career that saw its artistic climax when he was a man in his fifties.

Far more common are the artists who are forced to give up working, often years before their death, because of some kind of infirmity. Among the old masters, a well-known example is Piero della Francesca, who is reported to have become blind in his old age. While no documents giving his birth date exist, it is believed that he was born between 1414 and 1420, so that he must have been about sixty when he painted his last recorded work. According to the sixteenth-century author Berto degli Alberti, the lantern maker Marco di Longaro told him that as a small boy he had "led the master Piero della Francesca, the excellent painter who was blind, by the hand." However, after giving up painting, the artist devoted himself to the study of mathematics and perspective and wrote an important book on the subject. He died in 1492, at which time he is reported to have been eighty years old.

Another prominent artist who became blind in old age was Mary Cassatt, the nineteenth-century American artist, who was born in 1844 and died in 1926. After a brilliant career as the outstanding American woman painter of her time and one of the leaders of the Impressionist movement, she developed eye trouble and ill health in 1908, was partially blind by 1912, and lost her eyesight completely two years later when she was sixty-nine years old. Although she lived into her early eighties, she never recovered her vision, which had been completely destroyed by cataracts in both eyes. An operation in 1921 brought only slight improvement, and diabetes added to her discomfort. A querulous and vindictive old woman, she became increasingly isolated and lonely and died shortly before her eighty-second birthday.

Two other nineteenth-century American artists who had to give up painting in their old age because of physical or mental disability were Frederick Church and Ralph Albert Blakelock. Church, who was born in 1826, studied with Thomas Cole and became one of the most popular American landscape painters. His *Niagara Falls* of 1857, now in the Corcoran Gallery in Washington, D.C., and above all his *Heart of the Andes* of 1859, now in The Metropolitan Museum in New York, created a sensation and were viewed by thousands of eager people who paid admission to see these masterpieces. However, in 1877, when he was fifty years old, Church developed rheumatism, which increasingly crippled him so that he had to spend his last twenty years in enforced idleness at his Oriental villa, Olana, near Hudson in New York State. A photograph taken of him in his old age tells the story: "It shows the painter, aged beyond his years and bowed in body, grasping at the balcony railing with swollen hands as he looks down upon a street in Morelia, Mexico, his favorite winter haunt south of the border."[5] He died at seventy-four in 1900.

Blakelock's life and illness were of a very different kind. Born in 1847 and dying in 1919, his life was an unmitigated series of disasters. By the 1880s, when he was in his thirties, he had developed a highly individual style of Romantic landscape painting. He was exhibited in the National Academy and the Society of American Artists, but he received indifferent or damning criticism and had increasingly severe financial troubles, which were made more difficult because of his large family. However, as the *Collector* of December 1890 reported, "Neglected by the public which did not understand him; unnoticed by a criticism which dared not have any idea of its own; poor, burdened, depressed and often desperate, this man of ideals and vision never swerved upon his path." However, in

---

[5] D. C. Huntington, *The Landscapes of Frederick Church—Vision of an American Era* (New York: Braziller, 1966), p. 111.

1899, at the age of fifty-two, he suffered a severe mental breakdown and was hospitalized for most of the rest of his life. In 1916 when his health was somewhat improved, he tried to take up painting again but the venture was unsuccessful. Blakelock had a relapse and died shortly after at the age of seventy-two. Ironically, it was only during his illness that his work became recognized and that collectors began to buy his pictures.

There is one other phenomenon that is especially characteristic of the twentieth century, and that is the artist who is prevented from working because of his political or ideological beliefs. The first of the countries to practice this kind of suppression was the Soviet Union. Interestingly enough, in the early days of the Russian Revolution, Russian avant-garde artists such as Kandinsky, Chagall, Gabo, and Pevsner, were welcomed and given important commissions by the new Soviet state, but in 1921 this policy was changed. Lenin decided that abstract art was not in keeping with the ideals and needs of the new society and that Social Realism was the only proper form of artistic expression for the Communist revolution. The result was that most of the prominent modern artists emigrated to Germany or France. The only ones who stayed were Tatlin and Malevich, the latter the founder of Suprematism, who died in 1935 at the age of fifty-seven.

Vladimir Tatlin, born in 1885, was the very essence of an avant-garde artist and had been one of the leaders of the Abstract movement before the revolution. He had started out as a painter, but in 1913 he turned to sculpture and after discovering the work of Picasso and the Cubists, founded Constructivism. His major project during the brief period when the new regime favored modern art was the monument to the third Internationale of 1919, an extremely original and bold creation. When nonfigurative art was denounced as counterrevolutionary, Tatlin turned to teaching and ended up as a member of the Research Institute for Artistic Culture in Leningrad, specializing in the study of materials. After 1927, when he was forty-two, he was put in charge of ceramics at the newly organized state studios in Moscow, where he designed consumer goods for the proletariat. From 1929 to 1931, he was occupied with building an air bicycle called Le Tatlin, and the last thirty years of his life were devoted to designing a glider—which never left the ground—as well as making sets for theatrical productions. He died in 1956 at the age of seventy-one.

Equally oppressive was Hitler's Germany, where all adherents of modern art were denounced as degenerate, dismissed from their positions, and deprived of any opportunity to display or sell their work. In the very early years some of the Expressionists such as Nolde, who had been a member of the National Socialist Party long before 1933, welcomed the new order. Barlach was asked by Goebbels to make sculptures for the Propaganda Ministry in Berlin, but like Lenin, Hitler soon decided that modern art was too dangerous and too individualistic to serve the aims of the National Socialist movement. The result was that even those who had sympathized with Hitler and were neither Jews nor Communists were persecuted and suppressed, so that many decided to go into exile rather than endure the oppressive regime. Among these émigrés were such prominent figures as Mies van der Rohe, Walter Gropius, and Max Beckmann, but most of the leading Expressionists stayed, as did Käthe Kollwitz, the famous woman artist.

Kollwitz's experience was characteristic of the fate that befalls a creative artist under an absolute dictatorship. Born in 1867, she had studied in Berlin and Munich and in a short time became one of the leading graphic artists in Germany. A recipient of many prizes and honors, a member of the Prussian Art Academy and a teacher at the Berlin Art Academy, she was one of the most respected and best-known German artists both in her own country and abroad. Upon Hitler's coming to power in 1933, when Kollwitz was sixty-five, she was at once expelled from all official positions. Three years later, in 1936, she was forbidden to exhibit and finally prevented from working altogether. But she stayed on, enduring not only her own hardships but also the horrors of the war. As she put it, "I want to stay with the rejected and I must." At the age of seventy-eight in 1945, she died a few days before the end of the war.

 **7** *AND INTO THEIR NINETIES...*

*A*n increasing number of human beings live into their seventies and eighties, but even today relatively few reach ninety, and those who are sound in body and mind and still actively pursuing their profession are rare indeed. Yet reports of such people have come down to us from biblical and classical times, and while these accounts may be exaggerated or even legendary, there are many instances of modern people who not only lived into their nineties but were still active and making significant contributions. The most notable case in art was no doubt Grandma Moses, who, as I have said in an earlier chapter, put down her brushes only a few days before her death at one hundred one in 1961, having had the satisfaction of receiving praise and congratulations upon the occasion of her hundredth birthday the previous year.

Virtually all the artists whose activities during their nineties can be proved by documentary evidence lived in either the nineteenth or twentieth century, presumably because modern medical science has prolonged the life-span of men, and better care enables people to enjoy a healthier and more productive old age. Interest-

*Maria Martinez*
*Pottery Jar*
*1940s*
*Courtesy of Museum of the American*
*Indian, Heye Foundation,*
*New York*

*Today a woman well into her*
*nineties, Maria Martinez is still*
*making pottery jars similar to this*
*one.*

ingly enough, this seems particularly true of women, for several of the most remarkable artists who are still creating in their nineties are of the female sex. The most amazing is Maria Martinez, the famous American Indian potter, who remained vigorously active until the age of nearly one hundred. As *The New York Times* said early in 1977, "At 95, Maria Martinez seems to have no plans for retirement. The noted Indian potter, whose work is in the Brooklyn Museum, still keeps busy in her New Mexico studio and is scheduled to participate in summer workshops at the University of Southern California." Susan Peterson, in her article on Maria Martinez, describes her impression of the celebrated ceramic artist after visiting her workshop in San Ildefonso Pueblo in the following words: "At 92 she has fantastic energy: making pots, but only the size she can hold in her hand, and leaving them plain, undecorated now by anyone else, and signing them with her Indian name, Maria Poreka, greeting visitors to the pueblo . . . counselling her family in ceremonial and secular matters and preserving the traditions of the pueblo . . . speaking Towa to the young people, being in all respects a reservoir of traditional culture."[1]

[1] Susan Peterson, "Maria Martinez, Pueblo Potter," *Craft Horizons*, February 1970.

Two other outstanding women artists still active in their nineties are Georgia O'Keeffe and Sonia Terk Delaunay. The former, who lives not far from Maria Martinez in the Pueblo country of New Mexico, is no doubt today the oldest and most revered of American painters. Born in Sun Prairie, Wisconsin, in 1887, she can look back on an artistic career that spans some seventy years, starting with her student days at the Art Institute of Chicago from 1905 to 1908, and culminating with major retrospectives at The Museum of Modern Art in New York in 1946 and the Whitney Museum of American Art in 1975, as well as a magnificent publication devoted to her work in 1976. Today a woman of ninety-six, she is still painting. Critics have praised her recent work, seeing in it a further development of her artistic style, which was avant-garde when she first started exhibiting some sixty years ago and continues to be in the forefront of contemporary American painting. *American Artist* magazine in an article on her in 1976 had this to say: "Today, just 88, O'Keeffe still spends most of the year at the small remote ranch in the desert. She also maintains a more amply appointed residence in the village of Abiquiu, which she moved to after Stieglitz's death in 1946, but prefers the solitude and simpler surroundings of the ranch. She tries to have nothing in her house that is unnecessary, claiming, 'If you have an empty wall, you can think on it better.' "[2] And in 1977 an hour-long film about Georgia O'Keeffe at ninety showed her as alert and active as ever.

Equally remarkable, and somewhat older, is Sonia Delaunay who was born Sonia Terk in Kiev in 1885 and grew up in St. Petersburg. She studied in Germany and in 1905 went to Paris, where she settled permanently and met and married Robert Delaunay, the famous abstract painter who founded Orphism in 1910. She and her husband were in the forefront of the avant-garde movement of the pre–World War One days. During the 1920s she took up decorative arts and did not return to painting until the 1930s, but she emerged

[2] *American Artist*, January 1976, p. 86.

as a major artistic figure in her own right only after her husband's death in 1941. However, it was not until the 1950s and 1960s that she received international recognition as an important figure in the history of modern art. Delaunay's work was exhibited in a big retrospective at the Musée National de l'Art Moderne in Paris in 1964 and in other extensive shows in Canada in 1965, as well as in a second large Paris show in 1967. A major scholarly study devoted to her was published simultaneously in Paris and London. There can be no doubt that Sonia Delaunay, who died in 1978 at the age of ninety-three, was one of the outstanding painters of our age.

Another woman artist who lived into her nineties was Anna Vaughn Huntington, who was born in Cambridge, Massachusetts, in 1876 and died at the age of ninety-seven in Bethel, Connecticut, in 1973. Her long, very productive career extended over many decades, although her fame and importance declined as her more traditional, academic style of sculpture no longer appealed to a generation of artists and critics who were interested in more abstract modes of artistic expression. At her peak, however, she was greatly admired and given many awards and prizes. In 1936 the American Academy of Arts and Letters gave her a retrospective in New York, and another big exhibition was held at the Virginia Museum honoring her on her sixtieth birthday. In 1936 she was awarded the Widener Medal at the Pennsylvania Academy of Art, and in 1940, the special medal of honor by the National Sculpture Society. Her most famous works are *Joan of Arc* at Riverside Drive in New York, *El Cid* at the Museum of the Hispanic Society in New York, and her animal sculptures at the Brookgreen Garden in South Carolina. While she was less active in her later years, she was reported to have been too busy to take tests at a local hospital, which her doctor recommended in 1972 when she was ninety-five.

One who worked vigorously to the age of ninety-seven, until his death in 1982, was the Spanish-born American sculptor Jose de Creeft. A review of a 1975 show of his work comments on his ". . . undiminished emotional vitality and the striking technical skill which has distinguished his long career. A virtuosic direct carver of various woods and stones, de Creeft allows the particular qualities of the materials to inspire the conception of the sculptural form."[3] These lines were written when the artist was ninety, and afterward he produced many additional sculptures, chipping away with an energy and power that many artists half his age would envy. A film was made showing him at work, a new edition of a book about his art was published, and a large new exhibition of his most recent work was held at the Kennedy Galleries in New York.

Another leading modern artist who is still active in his nineties at the time this is being written is the Russian-born French painter Marc Chagall. One of the most famous of living painters, Chagall in 1977 celebrated his ninetieth birthday to wide acclaim. A full-length film

[3] *Arts Magazine*, June 1975.

*Jose de Creeft*
Amor, 1973
*1973*
*Courtesy Kennedy Galleries,
Inc., New York*

*This sculpture was done
by Jose de Creeft when he
was eighty-nine years old.*

was made for this occasion, showing the artist as lively and productive as ever. It is generally agreed that his most important
contribution to modern art was made early in his career when he
was a young man in his twenties. Born in Vitebsk in 1897, he had
just come from there to Paris. Chagall continued to produce a large
body of work. This work consisted not just of paintings, drawings,
and prints but of the stained-glass windows of the Twelve Tribes
of Israel made for a synagogue near Jerusalem, mosaics and a tapestry
for the Knesset, a ceiling painting for the Paris Opera House, and
large wall paintings for the Metropolitan Opera at Lincoln Center,
New York. Paul Stitelman, commenting on his 1974 show at the
Pierre Matisse Gallery, summarizes his contribution during old age

in these words: "Perhaps Chagall's greatest achievement is in consistently applying a folk sensibility to modern art, for in doing so he has delighted many to whom the advances of modern art seem incomprehensible—and there is certainly much to be praised in that."[4]

Just a year older than Chagall was Oskar Kokoschka, who until his death at ninety-two was still actively engaged in painting. Born in Austria in 1886 and trained in Vienna, he started his artistic career with a group of very expressive portraits, which he painted during the years just before the outbreak of the First World War. After serving in the Austro-Hungarian army and being wounded at the Russian front, he resumed his painting, working in an Expressionist manner. During the 1920s he turned to landscapes executed in a more traditional way reminiscent of the Austrian Baroque in their free and tempestuous style. Views of cities such as Paris, London, Marseilles, Dresden, Vienna, and Jerusalem showed the artist combining the Expressionistic aesthetic of the modern movement with a more traditional type of pictorial representation. During more recent years, especially after moving to England in 1938 and then to Switzerland in 1953, he tended toward ambitious allegorical and symbolic pictures, often with ideological themes, which most critics feel are less successful than his earlier work. Alfred Werner, writing on Kokoschka in 1976, had this to say: "Still at the rare age of 90 trembling in awe before the mystery of life, he made readable his vision, leading from one unfathomable world to another of unconquerable enigmas."[5] While Werner does not particularly like Kokoschka's late work dealing with allegorical and historical themes, which to him appear "too fuzzy, and weakened by their belabored symbolism,"[6] he nevertheless admires the immense energy and creativity of Kokoschka, who, despite many discouragements that left him embittered, continued in his nineties to produce pictures of a scope and ambition that is rarely found even in the work

---

[4] Paul Stitelman, *Arts Magazine*, January 1974, p. 71.
[5] Alfred Werner, "Kokoschka at Ninety," *American Artist*, April 1976.
[6] Ibid.

of artists many years younger. He was one of the last surviving masters of the Expressionist movement that played such an important role in modern art.

Several late nineteenth- and early twentieth-century artists reached their nineties but none did any significant work after his ninetieth birthday. Outstanding among them was the German painter and illustrator Adolf von Menzel, who was born in 1815 and died in 1905. A pioneer in introducing Realism and Anticipating Impressionism, he was one of the most creative and important figures in the development of German art, but his later work, while immensely successful, was less important in terms of the history of modern painting. By the time of his death at the age of ninety, he had ceased to create any important work.

Considerably older at the time of his death was the French painter Henri Harpignies, who lived from 1819 to 1916, dying at the advanced age of ninety-seven. A landscape painter who enjoyed a considerable reputation during his lifetime, he was a member of the Barbizon school and a follower of Corot, whose romantic style he adopted. As a young man he had traveled in Italy, but he painted chiefly at Fontainebleau and in the Auvergne and was famous for his depiction of trees. In fact, no less than Anatole France called him the "Michelangelo of Trees." In 1900 he won the Grand Prix at the Paris Salon, and in 1907, when he was eighty-eight, he received the Medaille d'Honneur of the Salon, but failing eyesight prevented him from working during the last years of his life.

A very different kind of artist was the American illustrator and painter Maxfield Parrish, who lived from 1870 to 1966. Although he had stopped painting some time before his death, he continued to enjoy considerable popular acclaim and was given a large retrospective at the Gallery of Modern Art in New York in 1965, when he was ninety-five years old. The exhibition aroused a good deal of interest in art circles. He died the following year at the age of ninety-six.

Turning from Western art to that of the East, there are a number of fine painters in both China and Japan who reached extreme old age and worked beyond their ninetieth year. The most outstanding is without doubt the modern Chinese painter Ch'i Pai-shih, who is regarded as the greatest Chinese artist of the twentieth century. Born in 1861, when the Ch'ing emperors were still ruling the Middle Kingdom, and dying in 1957, a decade after the establishment of the People's Republic, he was equally admired and honored by the artists and critics of Imperial China and the Chinese Republic as well as by the authorities of Communist China. Of poor peasant stock, he started his life as a carpenter and woodcarver and was virtually self-taught as a painter. He developed a very individual style, which was based on that of the two great eccentric painters of the early Ch'ing period, Tao-chi and Chu Ta, and he specialized in the depiction of insects, shrimp, fish, grasses, flowers, and bamboo.

Ch'i Pai-shih was an immensely productive and energetic artist. Although he was a man in his eighties at the time of the revolution, he became professor of painting at the Central Academy of Art, and in 1953, when he was ninety-two, was made president of the Peking Institute of Chinese Painting and head of the Union of Chinese Artists. It is estimated that he produced at least one thousand paintings and drawings a year, sometimes making a large number in a single day even when he was in his nineties. It is said that not a day passed without his painting at least part of the time, and that his artistic activity was intensified during the last years of his life, although the quality of his very late work was probably not quite as good as that of his earlier years. He worked to the very time of his death at the age of ninety-six in 1957.

Another Chinese artist who reached his ninety-sixth year—or by Chinese reckoning, his ninety-seventh birthday—was the thirteenth-century painter Chao Meng-chien, who lived from 1199 to 1295. He had a brilliant career as an official and scholar and was admired as the very model of a cultured gentleman who excelled in painting, calligraphy, and poetry. However, since he was related to the Imperial family, his career in government came to an end when the Sung rulers were overthrown by the Mongols, and he retired to

his native Chekiang province, where he devoted himself entirely to
his artistic pursuits. He is well known for his paintings of narcissus,
plum blossoms, and bamboo, and he wrote an essay on the plum
tree. While several of his scrolls survive, it cannot be said with certainty from which period of his life they come; but it is believed that
he painted into extreme old age.

Of the modern architects who reached ninety, by far the most remarkable was Frank Lloyd Wright, who died at the age of ninety-two in 1959. One of the greatest figures in twentieth-century architecture and a man of great personal magnetism, he continued to play an important role to the very end of his life. In fact, one of his most celebrated buildings, The Solomon R. Guggenheim Museum in New York, was completed only after his death. In his nineties, he was one of the most sought-after contemporary architects, and at the time of his death, many plans for new buildings were still under consideration on his drawing board. Wright's career certainly proves that an artist can still be a creative force and make a significant contribution in the ninth and even the tenth decades of his life.

The other two modern architects who lived into their nineties were the Belgian Henri van de Velde and the American Bernard Maybeck. Van de Velde lived to be ninety-four, having been born in 1862 and dying in 1957. An important figure in the development of modern architectural design, he played a prominent role first in Art Nouveau and then in Functionalism with buildings such as the Folkwang Museum in Hagen in 1900, the University Library in Ghent in 1936, and many other structures. He was also an influential teacher first at the Weimar Arts and Crafts School, which became the Bauhaus, and later as professor of architecture at the University of Ghent. His last important building, which he was still working on when he was in his nineties, was the design of the Kröller-Muller Museum in Otterlo in Holland.

Maybeck also was born in 1862. A California architect, he was a pioneer in the use of natural wood and in the introduction of elements of Japanese architecture into American buildings. His most important work was done during the 1910s and 1920s, but he continued going to his office until he was eighty. Even after retiring he worked on a project for a boulevard in San Francisco and made a model for the Unitarian Church in Berkeley. In 1951, when he was eighty-nine, he received the Gold Medal from the American Institute of Architects. He died in 1957 at the age of ninety-five.

# 8 THE CROWN OF LIFE

*T*he lives and careers of the artists discussed in this book clearly show that some of the greatest figures in the arts did their most profound and aesthetically successful work during their later years. This is amply demonstrated by two examples, the Cézanne exhibition held at The Museum of Modern Art in New York in the fall of 1977, and the Matisse exhibition at the National Gallery in Washington, D.C., which was shown during the winter of 1977–1978. The former concentrated on the work of the artist's last ten years, bringing together a group of deeply moving pictures which some critics regard as the culmination of Cézanne's art. The later was devoted to the splendid paper cut-outs which Matisse produced during his seventies and eighties when he was so physically handicapped that he could no longer do painting or sculpture. Perhaps the most moving instance of creativity in old age concerns the famous poem, called *Crossing the Bar*, which Tennyson wrote in his eighty-first year. "That is the crown of your life's work," his son said. Tennyson replied, "It came in a moment." A few days before his death, he said to his son, "Mind you put *Crossing the Bar* at the end of all editions of my poems." Surely, with examples such as these, no one can doubt that for some artists, old age ushers in a period of such fruitful creativity that it is, indeed, as Cicero said some two thousand years ago, the crown of life.

According to the 1980 census, more than ten percent of the American population is over sixty-five, which means that there are now some twenty-five million older Americans. Despite the increase, it is still rare for human beings to live into their nineties. A notable exception was the contemporary sculptor, Jose de Creeft, who attended his retrospective at the Kennedy Gallery when he was ninety-five years old. Even rarer are the people who live to celebrate their hundredth birthday, but the time may well come when modern medicine will make extreme old age much more common. Undoubtedly some of these people will be creative artists; the extra years of life and health will enable them to pursue their career for a longer period of time. One thinks of the many great artists of the past who died of diseases which today could have been cured. Had they lived longer, they might have produced masterpieces which could have surpassed anything they had done previously. This applies particularly to the many gifted artists who died before they reached their maturity, not to mention old age. And even some who lived into early old age, such as Cézanne, who died at sixty-seven of an illness which can now be cured, might have produced many fine paintings or sculptures if they had only been granted ten or twenty more years of life. Many others come to mind, such as Rembrandt, who died at sixty-three, and Leonardo, who was sixty-seven at the time of his death. That one can continue to develop even at an advanced age is indicated by Haydn who, when he was nearly eighty, said, "Am I to die now? And I have just begun to understand the wind instruments!"

In addition to mere physical survival, another factor which has a vital bearing on creativity in old age is the nature of the social and economic circumstances under which artists work. In this respect, primitive societies are probably best for elderly artists, since in these cultures, art is looked upon as a craft that is practiced by people who have acquired some particular skill. The greater the skill and experience of the artist, the more highly he is regarded. What counts most is the person's mastery of the medium, whether it be carving or painting, pottery or weaving. Under these circumstances, older artists would naturally continue to work as long as their physical stamina and health permit. A good example of this is at the Acoma Pueblo in New Mexico where all the most active and productive potters are old women in their seventies and eighties.

Of the more developed societies, those with traditional structures are probably the most conducive to the continuation of artistic activity in old age. With their master-pupil relationships and highly organized guild system, older artists and craftsmen retain a secure and highly respected position in society as teachers of young apprentices and as revered masters who are looked to for advice and as models.

A society which effectively sustained artistic creativity into the advanced years, at least for the scholarly elite, was Confucian China. There, as was pointed out earlier, it was the custom for people to retire fairly early from government service or other gainful employment and devote old age to the arts of painting, calligraphy and poetry as nonprofessionals. Some of these so-called amateurs produced masterpieces that are generally regarded as being among the greatest of Chinese and Japanese paintings.

In contrast to these societies, modern Western civilization seems to be especially hard on old people in general and older artists in particular, despite the better medical services available to them. With our excessive preoccupation with originality, emphasizing rapidly changing fashions in which one vogue quickly succeeds another, interest almost inevitably focuses upon the latest trend in art, so that the older artist who has found his own style tends to go out of fashion and thus is neglected or underrated unless he has reached a position of extraordinary eminence. The annals of modern art are filled with accounts of artists who could no longer exhibit or sell their work because with changes in fashion, demand for what they produced disappeared. Sometimes even well-informed people assume that an artist has long been dead simply because there no longer is a forum where his work can be shown and discussed. It is true that there were artists such as Bonnard and Morandi who went on working in their own style all their lives, and never lost their following of enthusiastic art lovers who admired and bought their pictures. But for every artist like that, there are hundreds of others who, although still producing fine work, are lost sight of long before their death simply because what they create is not in the style of the day. For such artists, old age is a period of great bitterness and often poverty, even if they enjoy good health and are still creative. Their public also suffers the loss of the opportunity to enjoy and benefit from these artists' work.

In his recent book on the Ulyssean adult, John A. B. McLeish makes the point that, in many ways, the creative life is more possible in the later years of adulthood than earlier life.

"It is essential to make this statement with force, even if it appears to be an overstatement, in order to correct at last the asinine convention in our society that creativity resides chiefly with the young and the 'highly-geared.' Being in 'high gear' is no guarantee that one will be creative—productive, perhaps. Assuming that a constant factor in all creative enterprises is the existence of certain personal gifts, talents, qualities, or self-actualized attributes, there then seem to be conditions or situations which set the stage, or help provide the soil and air—whatever analogy one wishes—for the creative enterprise.

"One is a release of time, not only to think but to rest and not think. A great forgotten truth about the later adult years is that many older adults, although they undoubtedly feel the constriction of time in the sense of remaining years, also have more time available, either through release from family responsibilities or through retirement or lighter work loads. . . . Thus the creative life is not only possible for men and women in the later years as when they were much younger, but in important respects often more possible. Nor does lack of money, nor chronic ill health, nor lack of family and friends remove these advantageous conditions for creativity in many older adult lives. They are still present even when one is naked on the shore."[1]

These observations, of course, are true not only for artists of great talent or even genius but for the many men and women who take up art as amateurs in their old age. And no doubt, as an ever larger number of people live longer and have more years of leisure

[1] John A. B. McLeish, *The Ulyssean Adult* (Toronto: McGraw-Hill, 1976), pp. 246–247.

because of early retirement, the number of old people who become involved in some kind of artistic activity will increase. Granted that Grandma Moses was a woman of extraordinary gifts and that few of those taking up painting at her age will achieve the kind of success that she enjoyed, nevertheless there will be an increasing number of elderly people who receive satisfaction and fulfillment from producing works of art. That artistic creativity of some sort exists in almost all people is clearly demonstrated by the spontaneous creativity of small children and by the general involvement of primitive peoples in whose tribes often every member engages in some form of artistic activity.

The many examples of artists who did their best work in their old age show conclusively that our later years can be rich and fulfilling if we continue to develop and utilize our talents and abilities, instead of allowing them to decline from lack of use. This is true not only for geniuses like Michelangelo but for all who enter the later phase of life in the right frame of mind. A good example is Mattie Lou O'Kelley, a Georgia farm woman who took up painting at fifty as a hobby and today, at seventy-four, is a famous and successful folk artist who is about to publish the story of her life. Although only a few will be that fortunate, thousands are capable of creating works of art which will give pleasure both to themselves and to their audience. Many an older person has built a house for himself or engaged in other types of construction that have given him a meaningful and rewarding outlet for his skills and creative potential. There are countless examples of old people taking up painting or sculpture, often with considerable success and satisfaction. Even more common are those who turn to crafts, such as pottery, textiles, basketry, metal or woodwork, fields in which it is possible to produce works that combine beauty with utility. What these elderly artists have to tell us is that we, too, in the last stage of life, can continue to explore both ourselves and the world around us. The wisdom accumulated over the years can be shaped into the crown of our own experience, for in the creative act itself we draw from the wellsprings of life.

# Bibliography

Badt, K. *Das Spätwerk Cézannes*. Konstanz: Konstanzer Universitätsreden, 1971.

Beauvoir, Simone de. *The Coming of Age*. New York: Putnam, 1972.

Chu, Ch'i-jung. *Ch'i Pai-shih, his life and works*. New Haven: Yale University Press, 1972.

Cicero. *On Old Age*. Translated by F. Copley. Ann Arbor: University of Michigan Press, 1967.

Clark, Kenneth. *The Artist Grows Old*. Cambridge: Cambridge University Press, 1972.

de Creeft, Jose. *The Sculpture of Jose de Creeft*. Text by Jules Campos. New York: Kennedy Graphics, 1972.

Dorland, W.A.N. *The Age of Mental Virility; An Inquiry into the Records of Achievement of the World's Chief Workers and Thinkers*. New York: The Century Co., 1908.

Gallwitz, Klaus. *Picasso at Ninety; The Late Work*. New York: Putnam, 1971.

Greenberg, C. "Picasso at Seventy-five." *Arts Magazine*, October 1957.

Grimm, J. *Rede über das Alter*. Reprint of 1863 edition, edited by H. Grimm. Kassel: 1963.

Jung, C. J. *Modern Man in Search of a Soul*. New York: Harcourt Brace, 1933.

Kallir, Otto. *Grandma Moses*. New York: Abrams, 1973.

La Fuente Ferrari, E. *El Greco—The Expressionism of his Final Years.* New York: Abrams, 1969.

Lai, T. C. *Ch'i Pai-shih.* Seattle: University of Washington Press, 1973.

*Last Works of Henri Matisse: 1950–1954.* Texts by P. Reverdy and G. Duthuit. *Verve,* No. 35–36, 1958.

Lehman, H. *Age and Achievement.* Princeton: Princeton University Press, 1953.

McLeish, John A. *The Ulyssean Adult.* Toronto: McGraw-Hill, 1976.

Marriott, Alice L. *Maria, The Potter of San Ildefonso.* Norman: University of Oklahoma Press, 1970.

Matisse, Henri. *Henri Matisse Paper Cut-Outs.* Text by Jack Coward, et. al. New York: Abrams, 1977.

Mosby, Aline. "Chagall at Ninety." *Art News,* vol. 76, Summer 1977.

Parmelin, Helene. *Picasso, Intimate Secrets of a Studio at Notre Dame de Vie.* New York: Abrams, 1966.

Parmelin, Helene. *Picasso: The Artist and His Model.* New York: Abrams, 1965.

Parmelin, Helene. *Picasso: Women, Cannes and Mougins, 1954–1963.* Paris: Editions Cercle d'art, 1967.

Peterson, Susan. "Maria Martinez, Pueblo Potter." *Craft Horizons,* February 1970.

Picasso, Pablo. *A year of Picasso paintings; 1969.* Text: Rafael Alberti. Translated by Anthony Kerrigan. New York: Abrams, 1972.

Picasso, Pablo. *Les Dejeuners.* Text: Douglas Cooper. New York: Abrams, 1963.

Picasso, Pablo. *Picasso, his recent drawings, 1966–1968.* Text: Charles Feld. Translated by Suzanne Brunner. New York: Abrams, 1969.

Picasso, Pablo. *Picasso 347.* New York: Random House, 1970.

Picasso, Pablo. *Picasso Variations on Velázquez's painting "The Maids of Honor" and other recent works.* Text by Jaime Sabartes. New York: Abrams, 1959.

Richardson, B. L. *Old Age Among The Ancient Greeks.* Baltimore: Johns Hopkins, 1933.

Rubin, William, ed *Cézanne, The Late Work.* New York: The Museum of Modern Art, 1977.

Simmons, Leo W. *The Role of the Aged in Primitive Society.* New Haven: Yale University Press, 1945.

Steinberg, L. *Michelangelo's Last Paintings.* New York: Oxford University Press, 1975.

Tannenbaum, Judith. "De Creeft—Kennedy Gallery—Review." *Arts Magazine,* June 1975.

de Tolnay, C. *Michelangelo. Vol. 5, The Final Period.* Princeton: Princeton University Press, 1960.

Werner, A. "Kokoschka at Ninety." *American Artist,* April 1976.

# Index

*Page numbers in boldface refer to art.*

## A

Acoma Pueblo, 205
Aix-en-Provence, 46
Albers, Josef, 158–160, **159**
Alberti, Leone Battista, 210
*Altersstil,* 7, 9, 11, 23, 26, 40
*American Artist,* 194, 198, 210
Archipenko, Alexander, 180
Aretino, Pietro, 14
Aristotle, 1
Armory Show, 175, 184
Arnason, H.H., 147, 165, 175
Arp, Jean, 162–163, **162**
*Art News,* 210

*Arts Magazine,* 196, 198, 210
Ashton, Dore, 73

## B

Badt, Kurt, note p. 47
Baldinucci, Abate Filipo, 29
Balla, Giacomo, 172–173
Barnes Foundation, 51
Bauer, G.C., 106
Beauvoir, Simone de, 5
Beckett, Samuel, 5
Beethoven, Ludwig van, 7, 18
Bellini, Giovanni, 96, **96**

Benesch, Otto, 29
Berend-Corinth, C., 63
Berger, John, 181–183
Bernini, Giovanni Lorenzo, 104–106, **105**
Biblioteca Laurenziana, 19
Bissier, Julius, 69–71, **70**
Blake, Peter, 143, 146, note p. 148
Blake, William, 118, 125–126, **125**
Blakelock, Ralph Albert, 189–190
Bode, Wilhelm von, 32
Bonnard, Pierre, 65–67, **66**
Brancusi, Constantin, 161–162, **161**
Braque, Georges, 150, **151**
Brighton Pavilion, 134, **134**
*Broadway Boogie-Woogie*, 155, **155**
Brücke, 176
Brunner, S., 210
Bulletin of the Boston Museum of Fine Arts, 37
*Burlington* magazine, 172
*Burning of the Houses of Parliament*, 40, **40**

# C

Cahill, James, 59, 91
Calder, Alexander, 163–164
Capitoline Hill, 19
Caravaggio, Michelangelo, 9
Carli, Enzo, 98

Carra, Carlo, 173
Carriera, Rose Alba, 112
Cassatt, Mary, 188–189
Cavalieri, Tommaso de, 12
Cézanne, Paul, 45–50, 203, 204, **48**
Chagall, Marc, 166, 196–198
Chao, Meng-chien, 200–201
Chardin, Jean Baptiste Siméon, 112, **113**
Chevreul, Michel, 7
Ch'i, Pai-shih, 200, **201**
China, 13
Chirico, Giorgio de, 169, 171–172
Christ, 15
Christianity, 21
Chu Ta, 140–141, **140**
Church, Frederick, 189
Cicero, 2–3, 204
Clark, Kenneth, 8
Claude, Lorrain, 109, **110**
Colonna, Vittoria, 12
Columbia School of Architecture, 148
Communism, 190
Confucian Teaching, 135, 205
Confucius, 3
*Conversion of St. Paul*, 14
Cooper, D., 210
Corinth, Lovis, 62–63
Corot, Jean Baptiste Camille, 126, **127**
Cotte, Sabine, note p. 109
Counter-Reformation, 21, 30
Craft Horizon, 193, 210
Cranach, Lucas, 100–101, **101**
Creeft, Jose de, 196, 204, **197**
*Crucifixion of St. Peter*, 14
Cutouts, 51–52

# D

Dadaism, 162, 175, 184
Dali, Salvador, 166
David, Jacques Louis, 122, **123**
de Kooning, Willem, 166
*De Senectute*, 2
Degas, Edgar, 128–130, 168, **129**
Delange, B., note p. 44
Delaunay, Sonia, 194–195, **195**
Della Robia, Luca, 103–104, **104**
Derain, Andre, 173–174
Descargues, Pierre, 34
*Die Kunst und das Schöne Heim*, 88
*Disparates*, 37
*Divine Comedy*, 126
Dix, Otto, 178–179
Donatello, 7, 23–25, **25**
Dorland, W.A. Newman, 6
Downes, K., note p. 111
Dubuffet, Jean, 166
Duchamp, Marcel, 184–186

# E

Eakins, Thomas, 131–132, **132**
Edmundson, William, 86–87
Eiffel, Alexandre Gustave, 187–188
Eilshemius, Louis, 186
El Greco, 29–32, **31**
Emmons, J., 29, 37
*Encyclopedia of World Art*, 114
Ensor, James, 169–170
Euripides, 3

# F

Fabos, C.M., 135
Farnese Palace, 19
*Faust*, 4
Fauvism, 173
*Feast of the Gods*, 97, **96**
Feininger, Lyonel, 158, **158**
Ferrari, E. Lafuente, note p. 30
Field, C., 210
Flexner, James Thomas, 186–187
Friedlaender, Walter, 107, 122
Fry, Roger, 47
Fuller, Edmund L., note p. 86
Fuseli, Henry, 116–119, **118**
Futurism, 172, 173

# G

Gabo, Naum, 163
Gabriel, Jacques Ange, 119–121, **120**
Gallwitz, K., 209
Gassier, Pierre, 37
Gaunt, W., 13, 21
Ghiberti, Lorenzo, 103
Gilbert, S., 67, 126, 130
Girtin, Thomas, 9
Giurgola, R., 9
Giverny, 42
Glaser, Curt, 58
Gogh, Vincent van, 171
Goethe, J.W., 4
Golding, John, 184–185

Goldwater, Robert, 42, 119
Goodrich, Lloyd, 130
Gowing, Lawrence, 39, 41
Goya, Francesco, 34–38, **35**, **36**
Grandma Moses, 82–84, 192, **83**
Grigson, Geoffrey, 169
Grilli, Elise, 55
Grimm, Jacob, 3
Grosse, Ernst, 69
Grosz, George, 178
Guardi, Francesco, 116, **117**
Guggenheim Museum, 143, 145, 202, **144**
Guiness, D., 121
Gyokuda, Uragami, 90–92, **117**

Hitler, Adolf, 191
Hofmann, Hans, 74
Hokusai, Katsushika, 55–58, **57**
Homer, Winslow, 130, **131**
Hopper, Edward, 155–156, **156**
Huang, Kung-wang, 136
Hugo, Victor, 7
Humboldt, Alexander von, 7
Huntington, Anna Vaughn, 195–196
Huntington, D.H., note p. 189
Huxtable, Ada Louise, 78

# I

India, 80, 147
Indian Pottery, 193, 205
Ingres, Jean Auguste, 122–125, **124**
International Style Architecture, 146–150
Islamic Architecture, 60–62
Israel, 80, 165

# H

Haak, Bob, 26
Haesaerts, Paul, 170
Haftmann, Werner, 68–69, 154
Hakuin, 142–143, **142**
Hals, Frans, 32–34, **33**
Hamilton, George, notes pp. 155, 159
Hamsun, Knut, 5
Harpignies, Henri, 199
Hartt, Frederick, 17, notes pp. 20, 23
Haydn, Joseph, 204
Heckel, Erich, 177
Hillier, Jack, 57–58
Hirshfield, Morris, 84–85, **85**

# J

Janis, Sidney, note p. 84
Janson, H.W., note p. 25
Jefferson, Thomas, 121, **120**
*Judith and Holofernes*, 24, 98, **99**
Jung, Carl, 4

# K

Kahn, Louis, 77–80, **78–79**
Kallir, Otto, 83
Kandinsky, Wassily, 153–154, **154**
Keller, H., note p. 97
Kerrigan, Al, 210
Klee, Paul, 71
Kokoschka, Oskar, 198–199
Kollwitz, Käthe, 191
Kondo, I., note p. 55
Konstanzer Universitätsreden, 47
Kramer, Hilton, 164, 181
Kupka, Franz, 175–176

# L

Lai, T.C., 210
*Last Judgement, The,* 13–14
Late Period of Picasso, 181–183
Le Corbusier, 145–148, **147**
Léger, Ferdinand, 150–152, **152**
Lehman, Harvey, 6
Leonardo da Vinci, 204
*L'Illustration,* 44
Lin, Yutang, note p. 3
Lindner, Richard, 71–73, **73**
Lindsay, Jack, note p. 45
Lipchitz, Jacques, 164–165, **165**
Lipman, Jean, 164
Lisboa, Antonio Francisco, 119
*Lucretia,* **28**

# M

Macdonald-Wright, Stanton, 179
Magnasco, Alessandro, 113–114, **114**
Maillol, Aristide, 160–161, **160**
Malevich, Kasimir, 190
Mantegna, Andrea, 98–99, **114**
Marc, Franz, 9
Marcenaro, Caterina, 114
Marchiori, Guiseppe, 53
Marriott, A.L., 210
Martinez, Maria, 193, **193**
Masaccio, 9
Matisse, Henri, 9, 50–53, 203, **51**
Maybeck, Bernard, 202
McLeish, John A.B., 206, 210
Medici, Cosimo de, 24
Mehta, J., note p. 79
*Memoirs of Giorgio de Chirico,* note p. 172
Menzel, Adolf von, 198–199
Michelangelo, 7, 8, 11–20, 21, **16**
Mies van der Rohe, Ludwig, 148–150, **149**
Miró, Joan, 165
Modersohn-Becker, Paula, 9
Mondrian, Piet, 154–155, **155**
Monet, Claude, 18, 39, 46, **44**
*Mont Ste. Victoire,* 48
Moore, Henry, 165, **166**
Morandi, Giorgio, 205
Mosby, A., 210
Mount Fuji, 56
Munch, Edvard, 170–171
Myers, Bernard, 177

## N

Nash, John, 133–135, **134**
National Socialist Party, 191
Nevelson, Louise, 74–77, 166, **75–76**
Nicholson, Ben, 89
Noguchi, Isamu, 166
Nolde, Emil, 153

## O

Odakane, Taro, 58
O'Keeffe, Georgia, 166, 194
O'Kelly, Mattie Lou, 135
Olmstead, Frederick Law, 135
*Opening of the Fifth Seal*, 31, **31**
Osthaus, Karl Ernst, 64

## P

Palazzo Senatorio, 19
Palmer, Samuel, 169
Parmelin, H., note p. 181, 210
Parrish, Maxfield, 199
Parsons, Betty, 72
Paul III, Pope, 12, 18, 20
Pauline Chapel, 14
Peale, Charles Wilson, 186–187

Pechstein, Max, 176–177
Peterson, E., 186
Peterson, Susan, 193, 210
Petit Trianon, 121, **121**
Picabia, Frances, 175
Picasso, Pablo, 9, 169, 181–183
Piero della Francesca, 9, 188
*Pietà*, 15, 21, **16, 99**
*Pinturas Negras*, 35
Poussin, Nicolas, 107–108, **108**
Primitives, 81–82

## Q

Quentin de la Tour, Maurice, 112
Quinta del Sordo, 34

## R

Ranke, Leopold von, 7
*Rape of Europa*, **22**
Raphael, 9
Rembrandt, 7, 25–29, 204, **28**
Renoir, Jean, 126–128, **128**
Rewald, John, note p. 45, 67
Richardson, B.L., note p. 3
Roberts, Colette, 74
Roberts, Keith, 172
Robertson, Giles, note p. 97
Rodin, Auguste, 132–133
Rohlfs, Christian, 63–65, **65**

Rolland, Romain, 13
Ronchamps, Notre Dame de, 146, 147
Rondanini *Pietà*, 17
Rothenstein, John, note p. 90
Rouault, Georges, 152–153
Royal Academy, 41, 117
Rubens, Peter Paul, 106
Ruskin, Jon, 157, 183
Russell, Morgan, 179

# S

Sabartes, J., 210
Sadler, J.T., 121
Sakamoto, Bishop, 60
*Salt Sellers*, 186
San Giovanni dei Fiorentini, 19
San Lorenzo, 24
San Quillet, M., 186
Santa Maria degli Angeli, 19
*Saturn Devouring His Son*, 36, **36**
Savonarola, Girolamo, 23
Sayre, E.A., note p. 37
Schapiro, Meyer, 48–49
Schmidt-Rottluff, Karl, 177–178
Scully, Vincent, 80
Seagram Building, 149, **149**
Sebba, H., 109
Selz, Jean, 171
Selz, Peter, 177
Sengai, 92–94, **93**
Sesshu, 136–137, **137**
Shakespeare, William, 1, 5, 18
Signorelli, Luca, 99–100, **100**

Simmons, Leo, 2, 210
Sinan, 60–62
Siren, Osvald, note p. 138
*Sky Cathedral*, 75
Slive, Seymour, 29, 32
Solon, 1
Sophocles, 7
Soviet Union, 190
Soyer, Raphael, 166, **167**
Ste. Marie de la Tourette Monastery, 147
St. Paul's Cathedral, London, 110, **111**
St. Peter's Cathedral, Rome, 18–19, 105
St. Peter's Collonade, 105, **105**
St. Peter's Lutheran Church, New York, 76, **76**
Steinberg, Leo, 15, 210
Stieglitz, Alfred, 175
Stratton, Arthur, 61
Suleiman the Magnificent, 60
Suleimaniye, 60–61
Surrealism, 162, 185
Swift, Jonathan, 5
Symonds, John Addington, 8

# T

Taliesin West, 143
Tamarind Lithography Workshop, 77
Tamayo, Rufino, 167, **167**
Tannenbaum, J., 210
Tao-Chi, 140–141, **141**

Tatlin, Vladimir, 190–191
Temple Israel, Boston, 76
Tennyson, Lord Alfred, 203
Tessai, Tomioka, 58–60, **59**
*Thirty-Six Views of Fuji*, 56
Tiepolo, Giovanni Battista, 115–116, **115**
Tintoretto, Jacobo Robusti, 101–103, **102**
Titian, Vecellio, 7, 20–23, **22**
Tobey, Mark, 156–157, **157**
Tokyo, 146
Tolnay, Charles de, 11, 17, 18
Treves, M., 42, 119, 130
Tung, Ch'i-ch'ang, 137
Turner, J.M.W., 39–42, **40**
Tyler, Parker, 127

## U

Ucello, Paolo, 97–98, **98**
Unité d'habitation, 146
University of Pennsylvania, 77, 78
University of Virginia, 121, **120**
U.S. Housing Authority, 77
Utrillo, Maurice, 174–175

## V

Valadon, Suzanne, 174
Vasari, Giorgio, 12, 13, 17, 20, 21, 24

Velázquez, Diego, 107
Velde, van de, Henri, 202
Vence, 52
*Venus*, **101**
Verdi, Giuseppe, 7
Versailles, Palace of, 121, **120**
Villon, Jacques, 67–69
Vivin, Louis, 87–88, **88**
Vlaminck, Maurice de, 173–174

## W

Wall Street, 76
Wallis, Alfred, 88–90, **89**
Wang, Hui, 138–140, **139**
Wang, Shih-min, 138
*Waterfalls of Japan*, 56, **57**
Water Lilies, 42–43, **44**
Weber, Max, 180
Weinmayr, M., 135
Wen, Cheng-ming, 137–138, **138**
Werner, Alfred, 198
Wethey, Harold, 30–31
Wildenstein, Georges, note p. 112
Wittkower, Rudolf, 106
Wood, Christopher, 89, 90
Wren, Christopher, 109–112, **111**
Wright, Frank Lloyd, 143–145, 204, **144**

# Y

Yale University, 77
Yale University Art Gallery, 78
Yonezawa, Y., note p. 91
Yoshizawa, C., note p. 91

# Z

Zen, 71, 94, 157
Zen Group, 71
Zen Painting, 93–94, 136–137, 142
Zurich, 161